Also by Bin Ramke

The Difference between Night and Day

White Monkeys

The Language Student

The Erotic Light of Gardens

Massacre of the Innocents

Wake

Airs, Waters, Places

Matter

tendril

tend

ril

bin
ramke

OMNIDAWN PUBLISHING
RICHMOND, CALIFORNIA
2007

Cover Image: Roman, Relief Panel, 1st century A.D.,
Stucco with pigment, 41 x 55 x 8.3 cm (16 x 21⅝ x 3¼ in.),
Gift of Mrs. Edith Healy Hill, 1922.4429, The Art Institute of Chicago.
Photography © The Art Institute of Chicago.

Book cover and interior design by Ken Keegan.

Offset printed in the United States on archival, acid-free recycled paper
by Thomson-Shore, Inc., Dexter, Michigan

Omnidawn Publishing is committed to preserving ancient
forests and natural resources. We elected to print *Tendril* on
50% post consumer recycled paper, processed chlorine free.
As a result, for this printing, we have saved:

5 Trees (40' tall and 6-8" diameter)
1,983 Gallons of Wastewater
798 Kilowatt Hours of Electricity
219 Pounds of Solid Waste
429 Pounds of Greenhouse Gases

Omnidawn Publishing made this paper choice because our
printer, Thomson-Shore, Inc., is a member of Green Press
Initiative, a nonprofit program dedicated to supporting
authors, publishers, and suppliers in their efforts to reduce
their use of fiber obtained from endangered forests.

For more information, visit www.greenpressinitiative.org

Library of Congress Catalog-in-Publication Data

Ramke, Bin, 1947
    Tendril / Bin Ramke.
        p. cm.
    ISBN 978-1-890650-26-1 (trade pbk. : alk. paper)
    I. Title
    PS3568.A446T46 2007
    811'.54--dc22

                                            2007023640

Published by Omnidawn Publishing, Richmond, California
    www.omnidawn.com   (510) 237-5472   (800) 792-4957
        10 9 8 7 6 5 4 3 2 1

ISBN: 978-1-890650-26-1

for

Melba Guidry Ramke (1917-2006)

and

Kenneth Michael Ramke (1943-2005)

CONTENTS

In effect, he is a mind bared to his environment, waiting on gods in a godless world

Julian Jaynes

AN ESTHETIC (ARS POETICA)

A window, this window onto my courtyard
where snow flies upward windblown; none
should assume beyond his own his isolation;

a lake is green, a local sky blues into gray,
any horizon darkens blue and green shades
into a wish, a wash of winter… it is snowing

which is a way out of his own silence; he feels
the abrasion of too many words flakes escaping
every mouth a whir a weather. "Beautiful"

someone said: aye, but buy, eat. Beauty
is as beauty used. Does its duty. Did. Used to:
be a duty. If to anagrams you add a letter,

a dull entry into the eager ledger, "beautiful"
becomes a form full of future, or could if
you would have it. Is a claim to future, a wistful list:

the history of future is a version, aversion is a kind
of aesthetic. As if. The beautiful is a form of that.
A clean room, a table, a window beyond, and beyond

that, green of trees and a lawn through the window
into the room the green of the room the air
the weather of the room of the lawn no the weather

underneath the snow the green of a past still
cool and quiet; a wall well woven into the mown
landscape is art, a wall made to be seen not used

scraped by air, wind snaking among long trees
loyal ally, long allée. Every sound its own silence
like light a shadow, Echo and Narcissus

home in their reflections still the lake
and the snow a wall of stone a long valley
visible from this window, the threatening

chlorophyll considerable against retina. Retained.
No one talks, no one about. About it they walk
in silence. If he needs to think he needs to think of

as in, "to think of the granular feel of light
falling into gardens this morning, this a light
insidious morning"; it may not be needed, nor desired,

this light this morning. "A world" the boy said
to himself—a kind of thinking, to say, as in, he said
to himself, "the world is bigger than I then thought,"

when the boy wandered into the garden among granular
bodies of light such a morning, this morning, that last morning
of his past, who was soon to learn a little future.

RESEMBLANCE

The rain is like itself,
broken pieces assemble resembling
a self; like mercury, the pieces roll in the palm, poisonous,
but that's not the point, they roll broken selves then
                              attach into one
shiny shapeless self, hurrah for heavy metal.
This night decants silvery into mind; some mind,
others rejoice, and mind is yet filled with light
                              and the light
dragged into view is yet filled with
("filled," of light, means vibrant) trembling selves
small and full of fear. If a young man murmurs
mainly to himself, fears himself more than god,
he hopes to protect himself from names with names
and maybe the occasional number.
                              The name
of the number is not the number.
Like a light explosive the night
carves its cavern out of such sight, leads
the sleeper frightened, lightened, or like…
                              the brain?—shall we
give it a name? Wait, one will come
to mind—waits for fortune to arrive unbidden,
the future perjured. Word versus word
as if the act of waiting mattered, made matter—
to matter, to make be where once wasn't—
spelled, to have cast a spell, to have spilled
                              magic into the
matter, not minding rational,
giving no reasons: but mind how I have seen
the shining glittered leaves in the morning
after such nights, the little spheres soon
to be vapor, a kindness of light refracted
through a temporary self of water. Glistening

17

strings of being
                        vast multitudes
of little shining webs and glistening strings....
                        (how interesting how
mere water manipulates the light, the light
bent and battered in morning drops
arranged for instance symmetrically)

Mind manners matters.
But that which matters is simply called
otherwise—called as in spoken to
in the sense cows are, or dogs which roam,
called home—pleasure, the mind minded.

TEA PARTY

There remain whispers. These were, are.

These are errors, terrors, he said. To himself, whispered.

[To Be Sad Safely]

A man named Henry Tuke in 1796 established a madhouse. His son Samuel (1784-1857) was interested in the conditions of the insane and wrote a book, *Description of the Retreat* (1813), which had great influence in reforming treatment. Samuel Tuke's son also entered the family business and aided in the management of the York Retreat, which became famous for Samuel's use of kindness and high tea, teaching his mad to indulge as the conventions required. When a patient could properly behave at tea, he was released.

There are so many uses of the mouth, the teeth and tongue—a portal of sorts, sorting the airy from the earth, the watery, dispensing and receiving in turn. We make of used air a sound and in turn speak, chew, swallow, choke, tremble on the glassy edge and hope we did it well, well enough, to enter the world, we would say. Like any creature trembling.

Trifles, truffles on the plate, seduction and a kind of medication, a kindness, can save us?

Thomas Wyatt (1503-1542) wrote:

That now are wyld, and do not remembr
That sometyme they put theimself in daunger
To take bred at my hand; and nowe they raunge
Besely seking with a continuell chaunge.

A word a small wind—notice
some outside my window,
beside some silence, appalls: white white
it might be saying, the words
                    I see move
a green limb, evidence of wind
winding through the glass
the window, wind eye, here beside me.

                        They flee
from me that some time did me
seek he said (I said of apparitions that they fly
when something comes, morning)
cloudless mourning. Dissipative,
susurrant, strange fashions for forsaking—

why it matters, whether matter enters—
Why it—Thomas, he was the doubter
and yet could be a saint in spite—
matters to take tea or not, perform according
to formula and not spill—enters—

and not fear and not fear.

Beside himself in various ways the world too much
with us who have passed the halfway point—like
leaves which do fall but not ill,

they accumulate in the fall, we rake them but
can no longer burn with impunity so the bonfire
of our children makes us wince.

                    Windows onto
something, the only thing the only sound
to penetrate: a spine of self and sound,
a spiral of hollow bones align a sort
not spill a thing anything will do, we
are such creatures

as dreams are spilled on. Nightmare,
lente, lente, currite noctis equi
someone sad said. Of?
It was no dream. I lay broad waking.

They fle from me that sometyme did me seke
he said and he was waking broad and loved
like anyone this life, he took what he could
and gave back more, was happy.
Why not.

[Enter Eros]

When her loose gowne from her shoulders fell
was there a man could see and not feel fall
the gown as if a curtain drew a slight aside
a sight a way it did it was and showed
a meaning for matter that was
beyond what was and could be later
when her loose gown from her shoulders fell?

And she me caught in her armes long and small.

But she didn't and it is fear I feel
falling from her shoulders like a gown
and flesh is falling from her shoulders like
a gown and fear is falling to my shoulders
like, shameful full of fury
my own head leaking the excretion
of my fear my dark shoulder showing
oh my silly fear will kill me.

To fear and fear and face it at the table
cup of tea in hand and others shoulder
to shoulder round we celebrate the day
the end the after noon with tea and say
the proper things and like to love each
the other apparition and despair desire
sitting on plates little cookies chew

21

there is fear to count on waiting humble
in our rooms to return to seek, bare of foot
and shoulder small and smiling all.

What is broken, what is whole, is
if you can touch it it will break. If it can touch you
it is whole. If it is it is, isn't it, or: we met
over tea on a veranda, looking out over—not
at each other, there was a landscape—looking out
over the steeply declined land and there
was a ribboned gleam below, of course, the course
of a simple river gleaming in the last of the lingering
sun, the kind of setting poems arise from, like mist
missed from the river which, in spite of its shimmer
is less river than rivulet, riven by land, the dirt declining
into, dissolving in, solving into itself. We resolved
never to taste that river, that water, water that was
has been so solved, so used to dissolve the lingering
issues of mist like a little landscape watched we did
didn't we, not each other but the little sun going we
watched sitting as we were side by side touching
(we cannot recall possibly our shoulders touched)
each the other, the warmth of the warmer one
draining into the cold or colder flesh of the other,
but we cannot recall and we no longer break.

SOCIAL CONSCIENCE,
WELL MEANT

He has a sly, a slight lisp. I eyeing him
notice his lack of symmetry.
Up and down
side to side mirror-like a lack.
Rummaging among ruins
he picks things up.

For a past he picks up what he can
to hold against the winds
the air as a place to be. Like a likeness
rather like the snail I leave this
trail shining ink or like the wound—
mute mouth the man once said—

no, like the boy with his stick trailing
against every fence paling following
himself in sound pointless palisade
of clicks like the typing but one likes
to hear. It is the act of portraying
the self which reveals, not the portrait.

When the paint dries it lies losing
luster chemically enervative
done with done for. The black billed
magpie lies fallen roadside black
and white and dead all over, unread.

Sounds like distance something to hear
in the night and the nation
derives from fear a self
and a settling, some word for winter.

"Pear" and "pare" and other doublings
play in the fearful boy's mind in the night
the light beneath the door a comfort
against lightning. The wind winds
its way down a hall

all waking in the night adds up
to a wound he is wound in the sheets
that tear, his tears he is a boy after all,
small. Sleep well, a deep source of darkness.

She said: Can you touch?
You can't, ouch! he said.
This kindly conversation, verse
contrary to the world's known anguish
tangible, a way to go and going, rejoice.
Her art was anguish, his a kind of kindness.
Sister and brother, child and child Piéta
                    Well meaning, this light.

SIX SCANDALS

Of the Sad Siblings

in sleep   in his sleep
the gentle madness   the ratios wound (wound)
in her sleep   into sleep

these weathers come   Kovalevskaya
to lift light   solved the case of a top
from the night   in which two moments
the night a word for it   of inertia at the fixed point

a small bird—*passer*—   are equal and double the third

passes her window and its shadow   when the center of gravity
across the drawn shade like a drawing is in the plane of
she would display   equal moments
she would play   of inertia (Whittaker, 164)

Of the Six-Starred Constellation

For it is the business of a man gifted in the word to prophecy
good. (Christopher Smart)

the light as a kind of passion   the spinning as of
a passing   the making of
a wilderness of bed,   threads and threats;
it lies above—   the toy survives the boy.

to wake is to wake
tormented
in her sleep
into her sleep

abed, a bed is a ratio
of threads and threats
sheets and blankets
a place to put

So with his sister he cast/he threw sticks
and read from I Ching:
Quiet perseverance brings good fortune
and each went separately softly to bed which is quiet
which is perseverance—to sever, no, *severe...*

sleeping daughter
is the cause

sleeping son
is the effect

of light
to enter again:
in her sleep
into her sleep
a dream of sparrows.

Of the Polydactyl Calculus

not rare but a surprise, that sixth digit
or there is one finger missing, and nine
digits indicates disaster, but such
as might engage and delight:
"For Nine is a number very good and harmonious.
"For Cipher is a note of augmentation very good.
"For innumerable ciphers will amount to something.
"For the mind of man cannot bear
        a tedious accumulation of nothings without effect.
"For infinite upon infinite they make a chain."

(Christopher Smart)

Of the Cat on the Sixteenth Floor

who that last morning was sitting,
the protrusion through the window, having
escaped the screen, and she (his distraught mistress)
was reaching through and begging him
to return and I being afraid I would distract
moved from the window and returned
to sleep with a vision of cat falling
without fear believing himself to have
the skill to land upon four feet
the art to right himself upon air
the right to live eight times insouciantly
the ability to not suffer gravity
but be borne on the back of all flying things.

Of the Birds of the Cities

PIGEON: which loves height and is not afraid
of the cat nor the foot of the passing stranger
yet does keep one eye cocked

CROW: which loves height and is not afraid
of the angry man whose fist is raised against
bird and god alike, who is late even before he awakes
for his appointments and his sinful anxiety

SPARROW/*PASSER*: which loves the low
places around the feet of diners on the sidewalks
and is aware of her name in Latin and her place
in various scripture and delights at the trope
of god's eye, of being the object of God's attention
even though she knows better and has always known
she was less than the crumb itself swept
by the hand of the waiter from the table.

Of the Six-Panel Korean Screen

Han'gel calligraphy, developed for farmers and women,
not the elegance of Chinese used by scholars:
the story of a man who played lute and his sister
who played flute and they were attended
by flocks of phoenixes…and after their death
he was lifted to paradise on the back
of a dragon, and she on the back of a phoenix
with fiery attendants of flocks in multiples
of six and sixteen.

"The bird alighted so softly it would crush nothing
would eat only dewdrops"

The left eye does not know what the right
eye is doing.

The eyes are not alike but are like
a sister and brother asleep in the same house.

GREGG SHORTHAND DICTIONARY

You must here imagine
the arranged swirls and swoops drawn
in a right-hand column, a group of printed
words left, for instance at a random page
Secretary, then
Sermon Serve Service Session
Several Severe Severity

Still, if you can dance, do. Unstill.
It was what her hands would do, did;
was this solace? Even the sad can dance,
given the chance. Half a chance.

It is possible no one now knows—does—shorthand,
strokes and swirls once ubiquitous accounting
for much and a hard life for girls.[1] She was one, this
one, good, and recorded every conversation
in her later life in Gregg, *solace*

is another word for later, being there. Her fingers
danced in her mind across a page making grace[2]
and notes; wantonness again:

Sewer Sex Shadow
Shall Share Shatter Shear
Sheathe Sheriff
Shepherd
Shibboleth

A little season, like solace, becomes the occasion
gently enough. Late and later.

---

[1] P. Bale, 1590: "The aret of brachygraphie, that is, to write as fast as a
man speaketh treatably."
[2] brachyycatalectic, *prosody* [cf. catalectic, GR....] missing a foot or two
syllables.

Pencilings:
in 1934, tested for speed and accuracy, my mother
placed second in Louisiana. Throughout her later
life she wrote, mentally, in her best Gregg—pencil

poised, a pad always by the telephone.
On birthdays, when I called, I imagined
the lines forming, the quick[3] strokes
not of her actual hands but of the hands
in her head she imagines as my voice.
Turning conversation into verse, returning

like drawing. It needs a pencil carved to particular
pointedness, a degree of sharpness. She practiced
sixty years in the privacy of her own caprice.
(from Old French *pincel*, from a diminutive of Latin *peniculus*
'brush,' diminutive of *penis*)

take, for instance, *obscure*: a left hand bracket,
angled, askew, a nipple pointing to eight o'clock,
and *obloquy*, elegant swirled cross-section like
eighteenth-century molding—ornamental
contours given to cornices.

Oh, and you should see her do
ecstatic—like a numeral 2,
and below it a small zero, or o.
Yet nothing written suggests
the rhythm of such writing,
the ecstasy in her moments.

---

[3] f. Greek βραχύ-ς short + -γραφία writing

Here are her stenographic pads, retrieved; I have
her own last Underwood, but transcription was trivial;
not like the slick feel of graphite scriptions,
hers alone, honed, with grace notes none
now can read without her.[4]

---

[4] But all such issues must be distinguished from mere brachylogy,
f βραχύ-ς short + -γραφία writing "speech": …conciseness of speech,
laconism; …a condensed expression, which was hardly characteristic
of the time or the family who had stories to tell and (so they believed)
time to tell them. But in regard to the issue of writing, recording,
concretizing the narration—this was a different order of being to
such as we were then, or could imagine being. We did keep things as
souvenirs, as minders of a time, reminders, of a time and place and of
moods and mediations, and such things—paperweights, ball-point
pens with addresses or cute sayings or depictions of nudes on the
barrels, sheets of embossed stationery from hotels we really could
not afford to stay in—for that matter, the towels which did carry
then the name of the hotel as claim to property on their side, as aide
de memoir on ours, thus stuffed into luggage—all these things were
what we relied on to provide shape and a (false) promise of continuity.
Meanwhile her name will be lost to the next generation since her only
brother died childless and they were the last, this brother and sister,
forming a sort of underline beneath which a sum could be inscribed—a
zero, if it matters [Latin materia (also materias) wood, timber, building
material, material of which a thing is made].

THE LAST DAYS OF GÖDEL

What counts in a life? If its end
is terror, this tendency numbers have to combine
into mind, to add themselves all unheeding
into the new, the no longer numerous.
Arithmetic is thought
to occur in the left cingulate gyrus.
A mapped brain a geometry: Mind,
a closed system, can know what it knows

of itself only by what it knows of itself. Gödel
showed we cannot know what we know.
No, what we don't. *Whose only wish was that*
death come as soon as possible
without causing any trouble to others,   Gaisi Takeuti,
his friend wrote. *There was no grief, no sorrow.*   *Memoirs of a*
What consumed him was such a nihilistic despair   *Proof Theorist*
that it could scarcely be called despair.

His brother Rudolf remembered the rumor
wandering ghostlike the Brünn Gymnasium
that Kurt committed no errors
in four years of Latin—a closed system   not only was his
complete, a sanctity—like the virtue   Latin given top marks,
inedia—begs to fill appetite, a failing.   but…he had made not
It was rumored   a single grammatical
                                            error   —Rudolf Gödel

He predicted his own death three times: in nineteen
forty-six, in nineteen seventy, and finally
correctly in nineteen seventy-eight. He starved
himself for fear of poisoning. When he walked
his feet would break through and find a falling.
Thin ice.

                    Attention wavers;
the water to walk on   glitters;
a wash of sun   on skin   a recompense
even as gathering damage warns—who doesn't
need warnings   ice is a grammar
a thin film on chaos, words, churning

in a past his little
triumphs glitter watery or mirage.
Beckon him back. A little life
was not enough, still he will not move
but feels a light
particular caress.

Furthermore, when his wife returned from his funeral,
a burglar had broken in and jewelry and other goods
had been stolen. I felt then
resentment against modern   Gaisi Takeuti
times as well as American society.

Consider a hand on your back:
his best hand takes your right hand and
both feel the day descend piece by piece
a cumulation of catastrophes
huddled in the light—

your skin exceeds you.
To have touched some skin
a skin upon itself then a body beneath
when we walk our feet break through and find
a fallenness: *who will live his life?*

His skin prepared itself
for proofs: geometry for the weak,
logic for the strong. A skin is surface.
Any page will do.

Making a science of my own bad mind
I learned to know a world, any world, again;
not as it could or should be but as a thing
of parts rewarding the one to piece a theory
but not back, not again, always afresh—
to be a big boy among little teams
and learn a means to quantify lack.

As proof they offer to learn a kind
of kindness, a drifting calculus
to interpret stones; among the numbers
only trust the average, all types of time

summarized and simulated, the appalling
will to know emergent, the felt recalling.

The thridde point of Theorique, Which cleped is Mathematique,
Devided is in sondri wise...The ferste of whiche is Arsmetique,
And the secounde is seide Musique, The thridde is ek Geometrie,
Also the ferthe Astronomie.   John Gower, Confessio Amantis

Do not leave the mark of your body in bed.
Never pluck a garland. Do not eat beans.
Avoid that which has fallen. Never stir the fire with
iron nor eat from a whole loaf. Do not eat the heart.
Do not walk on highways. Do not let swallows live
under your roof. When you remove a pot from the fire,
do not leave its mark in the ashes. There were many
rules for the Mathematekoi, who lived with the Society,
had no possessions beyond the body and learned from
Pythagoras himself.

What counts?

Luck and

in fall leaves turn charming colors
& maybe there is distance made visible

a physical thing like a future—

the long afternoon is a sin
of years on spindles,
a piling up mathematical out of legend,

the one about the end of the world

gold light settles onto the diamond needle;

an elaborated set, rules the luckiest learn.

What counts?

through your window watch
whatever falls
fall.

Herein lies his fame, his Incompleteness Theorem
which simply says If system S is consistent
we cannot prove it within itself; S and the proposition
"S is inconsistent" is consistent. The consistency
of axioms cannot be proved.

Herein lies his fame: he was a thin man
who distrusted food, which is to say the world
which was discontinuous with his body
and like any saint, S, would be unprovable
to himself his slender self infinitely regressing.

Herein lies his fame: he erased himself;
the null set, the sadness infinite and pale

After his death, his last days lingered in my mind.   Gaisi Takeuti
Why should the last days of Gödel have been like this?

PHARMACEUTICAL

In spite of the dark the sound
of his footstep comforts
there is light
there is time

I am on his shoulder and he is to me a machine
for moving me

the dark sound of his feet, my feet soundless
the shape of light

windows we ignore are rectangles
stars have no shape
windows we look through have no shape

If I were still the child I was

I recall the first time I read—no, heard Burroughs read
his account of a death from inside, an image of brain
as storm cloud with lightning diminishing
electric events of whatever dimension
grown brief, quiet, gentle. Implied danger grandeur
and distance. An uncontrollable element waits
in every human skull a kind of magnificence.

So into a long life I carry a brain like a child
on my shoulders, holding its little feet with my hands
to give it a nice view of the dark world passing.
The condition of brain: there's struggle between belief
in talking, and in taking drugs; an embarrassment.

Chemistry is control but when a mind
in the midst of the welter, when
the D2 receptors are filling up,
hovering between sixty and eighty per cent occupancy
levels, the mind-brain cannot know itself, or what to do

with itself, or whether it is a self.
It is a question and an answer, rider and ridden,
all questions and all answers simultaneous.
Is time as well as space, as is chemistry—
"event" is never simple no matter...
(Is there a smallest division of time? that
would be simple. The smallest period during which the smallest
piece of matter can do a thing—change. Assuming
a smallest division of matter.) Nothing
is prior to something, the boy said,
sitting sad on his father's shoulders. All once and forever.
So the little mind, called "brain" or "soul" or "self,"
is aware of itself enough to control itself
before collapsing into faith, or
prejudice, or superstition, or despair.

It is an amazing moment, to hear yourself scream with all
the authority of adrenaline, this in a white-walled room
furnished
with a bed complete with straps and cuffs as out of Kafka,
"Kill Me Kill Me Kill Me Kill Me Kill Me..." until
the meds take effect.

How the mind can frighten itself: can the mind frighten itself?
Like a cat turning sideways to his reflection, appearing to be
larger than he is, puffing up into something scared and scaring?
Is that a self? he said sighing.

Flesh melts
not pretty   I among others
leave to you grave
a grave consideration

and I have not prayed in this life
time but don't suppose it would
hurt to try   it always
hurts to try   he cannot not
believe in a life to come while I

cannot   he was cheated
of this life and it needs replacement

and pray   suffer
under the weight
in a place of replacement

I rode on my father's shoulders
like Christ who did not we now
know ride the shoulders of
Christopher called Saint
who was not neither did he die

the aisles blaze yellow bright

later we take together
a cup and balance something
against something   drink
together ceremonially but also
we like it

in his brain seventeen
long notes an escape
embraced passes be
fore anyone can feel
home a place beyond:

damage
or be damaged
as if there were options.

YEATS WAS ASKED

To write a poem about the war,
can you tell the casualty from the cause?
An angular descent of light
then it is a new year
very like the old year
yet newly named. Colder.

Still the light descends, eight minutes
from the sun (more or less) a gift.

We open our dictionaries for the morning
service, and some intone the definitions,
and some the parts of speech, but the wary
huddle among the shadows
to mumble etymologies.

(*Romanic-speaking peoples, who were obliged
to avoid the Latin* bellum *on account of its formal
coincidence with* bello- *beautiful, found no nearer
equivalent in Teutonic than* werra)

This is a new year when
we kiss and make up:

(werran, *whence modern G.* wirren, *wk. vb.
to confuse, perplex; the earlier vb. survives
in* verworren *ppl.a.,* confused, *f. Teut.
root* *werz-, *wers-, *whence also WORSE a.*)

The inchworm moth is of the family geometridae—
geometer, earth measurer. The inchworm
merely moves himself and has
arranged through time his feet
into small groups, front and rear. He also
emits a thread of silk (a thread of self)
and can when so inclined divide

himself from touch to dangle
dependent upon air, to twist into
safety singly, small; like a song he rides
air and will fall again lightly.
Like light to fall upon a leaf or blade.

Why is there weight?

Couldn't even we have designed a world
of wishful movement lithely timed
minus this gravity which grinds
us into selves?

When Georgie met the great William
he was then shrinking starlike
over longish time—thirty years
her senior, he wrote silken
lines, liked to land on his gathered
feet—becoming cold and dense and still
credited with light which began its
journey in a brighter time. What
we do does persist, hardening
into grains, annoying into pearl.

This became his geometry: her breath
in the night next to him, both breathing
because they couldn't help it. Breathing
beneath each language, not a word
spoken without the hiss and whirr:
there was a war, always is.

A HISTORY OF LEISURE

That which passes with no lesson learned
a ghost neither feared nor frightened
an emptiness anechoic colorless forlorn
awkward this language with no better word
than empty too few syllables too little
history no drama or minor, yes

so I offer a little emptiness which
looks a lot like a begging bowl
I demand neither coin nor attention
or maybe attention yes a little but
not for my sake but to show
a lifetime can come to something

I only ask that you look I speak
from no place utopia a void a word
is its only home you do not live here
it is only home home and I am here
I never left I am full of regret
I am always hungry (cf. *Ghaki*)

æmetta leisure plus *–y*
the vowel of the middle syllable æ- *meti*
was dropped in Old English the initial æ
being shortened yielded as usual in Middle

English dialects the parallel forms *ā* and *ē*
hence the forms *amti* and *emti* the former
died out in the fifteenth century the latter
with the euphonic p normal between m
and t is represented by the modern form (OED)

if I am nothing I do yet matter more
or less lyrical against the weight
the wilderness of matter euphoric

and distance is nothing to me
your pain is nothing to me
your desire is nothing to me

your happiness is nothing to me
your season such as spring with its
brittle birds and brilliant foliage
is nothing to me your season
such as winter with its enfolding
forms of water and they glitter
like air made
heavy into clarity

your empty gesture
into the future called art
you're the last
of your kind you're the first

of the curious races of men
to be satisfied with something
anything as long as it can
be felt against the skin; it
vibrates in the wind

PERFORMING ART

To name the air or the vapors clinging where
are ghosts amid caravanning clouds
anyone could see who cares
and anyone did see who declared interest:

wonder as wisdom circumstantial
such as when the prince abandoned
Rusalka for the foreign princess (soprano)
[here follows a name, complicated]
Prince and Rusalka die because she
repents of what sin she is assigned
by whom a human soul she dies
Prague, March 31, 1901, music
by Dvorak libretto by Kvapil
thus naming the air or the vapors clinging.

I don't know where this conviction arose,
mine, that beauty is chiral, left or right
handed a spiral of aspiration engaged
in some accidental glory some substitute
for glory at least   she
for instance, see her as someone, or two—
every body doubled as the grass is the rain
itself embodied (she is embodied)

and the sun
                    and as the grass
is the color of rain and sun   and
the body and just as the body of grass
is the wind
                    engaged broken into
exponential selves the wind
is the breath of the grass grateful
for the light

                    and just as the face
of your beloved is turned away
from you glorious on
the other hand
                    here is history: you
reach with your left hand out to touch
the right side of her face and turn
her not toward you but toward
some vision of grass some

vision of air of sunlight which is
not yet outrage but is knowledge
the mirror turns you back symmetrically
odd a right-handed self responds

your sinister gesture and the long
night continues dayward   the house
the mirrored self in the window   out
is dark in is light, the room,

                    interior burning
the mirrored self surrenders easily
does not bleed unbidden will not anger
until provoked is merely
to mirror is to succumb

"An image may also be transmitted from mirror
to mirror, so that as many as five or six images
have often been produced. For whatever lies hidden
behind in the inner parts of a house, however tortuous
and secluded be the ways in between,
may yet be all brought out through these involved
passages by means of a number of mirrors and seen
to be in the house. So truly does the image shine
across from mirror to mirror; and when it has been
presented left, it becomes right again, then

once more it comes back again and
returns to the same position."
(Lucretius, *De Rerum Natura*, 4:302-310)

like having a child or any copy
a betrayal ("an elaborately made fake book
for a New Year's present described
in the Duke's inventory as a *'livre contrefit*
d'une pièce de bois en semblence d'n livre
où il n'a nulls feuillet ne rien escript'

book made from a piece of wood
to resemble a book, with no pages
and nothing written in it" (footnote
to Michelle Boisseau's "Two Winter Pictures")

a poem in a book reflecting
never ending: Boisseau between wood *bois*
of the fake book which contains nothing
and bushel, of cooperage, containing
and *boisson*, drink…two pictures winter…

but a wooden book contains wood
the real book contains

                              nothing
only words   she had a way with
words   ) away with words
there is no interior

                      mirror or not
to open is to make exterior   No
to open is to make the inside the out

consider disease   (the circumstance
is no longer allowed) its use and is
like youth to be endured and among
the strong surpassed

                         we call it
bad   (to indulge disease its fond
aftermath)   faith
                         yet every adult
does envy the school child lingering
malingering after measles—measly
spots—regretting
                    nothing
                                   Jacques
later James Tissot painted "A Convalescent"
by the large pond in his   later Alma
Tadema's   London garden the long

convalescence a Victorian luxury
the envy of the conquered world

indispensable to Empire   he completed
the painting the year of the first performance
of The Ring at Beyreuth   the second year
of Impressionism   while Schliemann

was still laying waste Mycenae
in search of Troy   a woman
convalescing warms
within sheets shrouding

wafting atmospheres with each turn
of limb and torso   my friend's
project was drawing her love   her lover

asleep
                   she would set her alarm
clock for three   she would upon waking
gather materials to walk through darkness
to his house   to let herself in with the key

47

he grudgingly gave   it is painful to look
she would leave after an hour
to draw   to erase
to make marks on a page
to darken the white page

I am only imagining

some sounds entered
from the street as   drifting
she felt cloudlike wandering
(the brain a cloud)

this man his manner and terror
she hoped for long stillness

he would turn and face the wall
at other times bury his face
in pillows she would not reach
with her right hand

would not touch   at other times
he'd lie so offensively looking
inward she could not remain
would end early to return

to her house with its cat and light
and another set of sounds
another window open against

her act unbearably kind   to feel
penciled points aligning
outlining   entering my face
a bright intervention.

...for the illness is not a catastrophe but a dance out of which new constructions of sensibility may already be arising
Enrique Vila-Matas

PROTEIN FOLDING AND ENZYME CATALYSIS

These were words, words not wind. And maybe
she did suffer, words, like geometry a word
and a way to mean, toward knowing and being,
this measure of earth. For instance, squaring the circle,
doubling the square, bisecting the angle, (any doing

with compass legs open revealing, the point
punctured the desk top the languid legs lean)
Polyhymnia was muse of geometry as of sacred poetry,
and of mime—but isn't any muse a muse of mime—
and of agriculture and meditation. Many songs.

She is often depicted veiled.
"…when she takes up a mirror and spreads her legs
to begin exploration, she will have to part
subtle folds and upon doing so will discover
a multi-layered object that opens and reopens"

Christopher Bollas, *Hysteria*
"The self looks inside its body…questions arise
about whether the girl wishes to explore x (any potential
opening) that sponsors derived questions such as
whether one would or would not wish to look further.…"

Mitosis is an opening, a ripping, from the Greek for thread,
mitos. Threads part, seam ripping, opening into.
Many songs, and inside the various seeds scattering
all kinds of proteins, beans, and biologies.
Her anguish is not ours, nor do we suffer who hear

her muted cries. A little prayer flares into mind (derives from
muse?)
Flares into Mind amusing, burning burning
it hastens to reassure; one of these, those days,

superfluous days. See,
it is fall already, or if not
it could be pretended, mimed: harvest
crops of Russian thistle, Amaranthus,
and Goosefoot, which did not

blossom but did dance, demure
into the season. All that chemistry
in there, all that unstable carbon, hydrogen, oxygen,
and nitrogen, with a little sulfur,
of the fields. Little lilies and birds of the air.

All made of something
and so few explanations.
So Jonah watched sunsets behind Nineveh,
was not content with its orange glow glistening off cisterns,
off tiled roofs and shiny surfaces—blood and fire

his sullen desire, not content with surface nor
with a drowsy season—the translator
gave us "booth" for where he sat, his hut he made,
this hovel I imagine and I imagine nothing
makes a prophet more angry

than his good God's failure to punish
as promised
the sun does not rise but we move
on our little earth's surface to meet it,
like a unicorn on the carousel, around

until line of sight includes the sun—
one of the symmetries of this rough world.
God is not amusing. God is asymmetrical.

GOVERNORS BEYOND THE RIVER

That river I lived along had a history
if not a name. But it had a name.
Such trembling utility it displayed
under the sun and under the wilderness
of insects bewinged and bewildering.
I did as a boy collect the abandoned teeth of alligators.

There is no time like the present.

Like a little boat time on the river wafts
like a little. And betrayal. Don't forget.

Minor flagellations in the night, along
the crumbling banks of the river. The crumbling.
There would be yellow light then lozenged
into the wilderness of out, outside, adventure.

ANIMAL INTELLIGENCE

We think they are *serene*, as in what we think we want
from weather: *serene* derived from dry, sere—
a dry mind amid mountains. A kind of minding.

Ghost is a guess of anatomy, a moderation of flesh—
the wet flesh renounced, repulsed—and a lover
returning home during seasonal darkness

creeps warily, wound up, wounding flesh,
this battered better self become, becoming hard;
hard to say why he so loved sadness, the equivalent

of evening, only the glancing light which goes
by many names crepuscular but not enough to read by,
only to linger. This is so maddening about dreams,

the sanity all called to the waking side, the sleep
a sacrament, a sly response or inebriate virtue,
a tantalus of call and response. Wound this way,

a tightened tangent of anguish, a dream
ascends into consciousness: some claim to
remember, others make it up

watching your eyes for signs.
Some claimed to dream grisaille, (black
and white vision invented by photography (about

the time dreams became symptoms) black
and white the boundaries—I would draw my
dreams with crayon, pencil, charcoal,

about the lover returning home into the mountains one dry
evening. *For instance, a lead animal will stop to look at a moving
chain and move his head*

back and forth in rhythm with its swing. He isn't concerned about
being slaughtered: he's afraid of a small piece of chain that jiggles and
looks out of place. Temple Grandin, *Thinking in Pictures.*

The woman explained to me
that I wanted the praise only of strangers—
my own crowd never enough. Good enough. No,

she said, You never ask for fear of getting.
She faded ferocious. Wounded.
It wound about itself: caduceus (a symbol

of course but also snake. A pair of snakes.
DNA-like twined night and day and delirious
with it within it.) A sound, another pianoish

dripping—(paired parentheses like snakes?)
wintry, sun a glitter of ices—or summer,
an agon of music like anger, water,

singular a nobility, of patience.
Another ghost is a kindness.
Recognition of one's kind

the wise call generosity. It is
to join of your own group…
ghastly, a pale demarcation of season, ending.

"As a child I fell ill of hunger and fear"
said a child who felt anger and cheered
himself with a gang of toys, a group—

Whose child is full of fear?
                    Weather
like distance, like choice—
some word for winter. *Conscious*, the word,

55

derives—from *rivus*, stream, and from
from—from words for knowing and
for *cut*.

       To segment the sky, the ocean,
the vast plain of mind, human, latitude
and longitude, x and y, street and avenue—

thus the goose crosses some grid
into some other grid, unaware of himself as
I would make him, glorious and serene.

Dry smoke drifts and turbulence cleanses
the memory (the fair emergency of trauma
the emerged mother,) smoke drifts turbulent

if gentle, winding clearly among the fictions
arising from the smolder the wreckage,
rising little soldiers, factions among the fortunes.

SYMPATHIES

How Art differs from Life: Diane Arbus: I think it does,
a little, hurt to be photographed. Or: One can suffer
from another's hunger: to be eaten.

For instance: I may be moved to tears over Io,
the account from Ovid, by such a sentence: *When she strove*
to stretch out suppliant arms to Argus, she had no arms
to stretch: and when she tried to voice her complaint,
she only mooed. she would shy fearfully at the sound,
and was terrified by her own voice.

Some are moved to laughter at the word *mooed—mugitus.*
All are chastised by laughter, by sympathy, by cows.
All flesh is grass, all cows eat grass, and every good boy
deserves favor. When something called "terror" happened
in the neighborhood some said we will never be the same.
But we had never been the same, and the ordinariness
of terror is who we are and were. Picture the glamour,
the shattering of the expected face in the mirror,
the pond's surface glimmering stirred by the breath
of the face facing reversed itself, leaning downward to drink.

I like the light of an evening, the way it quietly curves
around itself, settling. As the cows come home. These

capacities we have for comfort most disturbing.
How can you sleep knowing others are awake?
When does the sound of your own voice soothe?

Sleeping to the murmur
of our own little mooing,
just look how quiet we can be.

(these rains which come in the night
and lift the light from the bed
cause it to hover above itself—

to wake into it is to sleep doubly
and to know the cause of the light
is to enter again and only first-causes

a wilderness of shame supports any body
any boy poor in his sleep his gladness
pulled tight to his neck to protect

against the hours prepared to pass
solemn as bears trained, tormented
into gladness into indifference

the rain is an aid to sleep
only if the roof is sound)

Among the delights: tree bark's
texture like thick paint drying
needles, leaves, boles, buds, birds

and each has a name or
so we are told each tree is above
pleasure beyond yet we live among them

it was not as if we ran out of things
to name—clouds for instance
which alter—

we could label each if temporarily
there's no reason not to name children
or clouds or trees in spite

of how each can break any
limb or promise in their names
heroic and Latinate or coyly suggestive:

spruce, related to Prussia, a tree
and also a neatness; Black Locust
ominous plague-sounding name

of a delicate-edged grace;
they are dangerous, the names
and wood is alive in lumber as in limbs

or maybe here is why we love them:
they never apologize
never forgive   how human

they never were green in
one season, gold in the next, some—
others refuse, remain green to the death

like pets with tags we might collar them
train them to our attentions
they yet will ignore us, our names.

ECLOGUE

But gently tooke, that vngently came.
The Shepherd's Calendar, February

I have only a life. Essentially internal, a life,
as we say, of the mind…but it wasn't. I was
a body, a boy not in a body but like you I was

a body and mind which are, is, the same, a life,
and never you nor I knew how to live that body,
that life. How not to. We lived along bodies

of water with various names such as bayou,
coulee and swamp and marsh and river
and near us someone grew rice where

during the season a flood formed and we
lived in dense air air as a form of water
and we walked on ground which was infested

with the memory of water, land which oozed.
Oozygotic. Some dead Greeks observed
such ground and it teemed and they thought

life emerged spontaneous of wet earth
and from dead bodies. The dead give birth.
I have seen it happen.

Some are alive who believe that Hopi has no past
or future tense, also that the Eskimo—there is
no such language, but let's say some dialect

of Inuit—has a hundred words for snow.
They are wrong but we know what they mean.
The child often thinks there will be a word

for anything, everything lurking. And I
often thought the words I heard
such words must have meaning, even "snow."

To me. A thing, a condition, in pictures;
on my coast it hadn't happened. Not to me.
I have no story to tell. We of the South

tell stories, I'm told.
I had stories
of the uncle who killed

a borrowed mule...the way they told it
was funny. It was not. He killed
a mule his stupidity and stubbornness

incurred a debt his nine brothers and sisters could not afford
during the Depression but
wantonly killed a peaceful animal who had—

here is the joke—neither pride of ancestry
nor hope of posterity. An old joke.
All the stories need not be told.

Another uncle threw a piano into the river.
I don't know why, hadn't the heart to ask.

It was my recurring fantasy to gather
lightweight staples—there were books
about such things, to keep cowboys alive,
and sailors—and fishing hooks and lines
and purification tablets for water—and
I had repaired the boat in our backyard,
planning to spend months moving upstream
in the shade of the palmetto and cypress
which lined Adam's Bayou a hundred yards
from our yard but which might lead somewhere,
any elsewhere. I knew better but it was
still my little daydream. I knew real boats

because of uncles. One who steered his elegant
wooden hand-made boat, his hands,
through the channel into the Gulf of Mexico
while the sun was just rising, and the Gulf
and the boat and our hands were the color of shrimp.
We would hand-over-hand distribute a net,
with great weighted boards which he told me
would ride upright along the bottom to keep
the mouth of the net open as we trawled. Traveled.
We poured back the trash-fish, as silver as any we kept.
As elegant. All that was real was not enough, not lonely
enough, not adventure, as if out of a book.
But to float alone along the dark bayou
living off fish I would catch and water I would clean
was official adventure.

I cannot be consoled for never knowing my own
my adventure. *She smiled with sober cheer,*
And wish'd me fair adventure for the year
                    Dryden's translation of Chaucer.

All nature listens silent to him, and the awful Sun
Stands still upon the Mountain looking on this little Bird

That's by Blake. "The Lark's Song." We
had no lark, no mountain. All Beauty
was elsewhere, in places with mountains and larks.
I read nowhere about bayous, coulees, or
rice fields (flooded during the growing season harboring
larvae of mosquitoes and flooding the homes of crawfish,
fields soon to be prowled by monstrous machines),
or swamps as Beautiful (cf. *sublime*)
nor read much of anything about such places ever.
The only rivers in writing were clear, cold,
and fast running, never the sluggish creatures
of my neighborhood, that dismal dream.

farewell Love and all thy lawes for ever,
Thy bayted hookes shall tangill me no more:
So sang Thomas Wyatt.

If you lose the boundary of your own life you must
experience everything. Here were the old Greek
madnesses, four of them: Prophetic madness due to
Apollo. Ritual madness, caused by and dedicated
to Dionysus. Poetic madness which is possession
by Muse, and Erotic madness which is...obvious
and not unknown to farmboys.

Paranoia, *para* plus *nous*, mind...a parallel mind,
a second mind, being of two minds, being overly
mindful, mind your manners: minded matter.

Farewell Love and all thy laws for ever

...lest anything should impede his momentum, he would
let certain things pass unfinished; others he propped up,
as it were, with lightweight verses, joking that they were
placed there as struts, to hold up the edifice until the solid
columns arrived.

The Bucolics *he finished in three years.*
Aelius Donatus, *Life of Virgil* tr. David Wilson-Okamura).

DANGEROUS PROFESSIONS

A certain place where people lived they
watched an Army train parachutists while
the people would watch during summer
afternoons the silk cups the white cups
inverted descended a blue sky rising beyond
them refusing to be guilty the sky displeased
when the parachutist first falls then floats it
is unnatural the sky retreats farther into blue
above white silk and airplanes and us
who merely watch falling.

A better word for those who float
dangerous out of the sky, against the
light seen floating dangerous down to us—
it starts with *A. ...Angels?* ...

Apple can make no promise wake as it will out of
seed—the word is heterozygote, a plant which
will not grow true from seed—into singular
new self as if willfully but no will is involved
invoked on Being beyond us we who watch and
would pluck and eat who would have the new
fruit hang tempt already full tight-skinned sweetness
not always a virtue dripping with human. William
Tell. Eve etc. The witchery of poisons in any
child's book.

                                        "Death from
Above" they wrote on their shirts—tee shirts
of the Special Forces, soldiers who fell
from the sky. Not fell,
but fell floating—what force
they felt how fiercely. It was
a way to be in the world, and change it.

Oh dear. Watch them walk awkward
on this earth, fearsome. Finding
a place for their boot heels.

A word here, a bit of breath...

At the end it's a quaint, querulous world
full of green trees and yellow earth you
will not remember their names or habits—
various Quercus will die unmourned,

as if it matters—"matter" as a verb to make
anguish into leaf and leaf and another leaf. They will glitter
up there without us, turning in wind during the days
and the nights alike.

At your end your last lasting contribution
would be to pronounce the names again, once
and honorably. The last love and lingering.

A tale, not my own, began: once upon a time there was a child
who was willful and would not obey her mother. Because God
took no pleasure in her, He caused her to sicken and die.
When she was buried her arm came out of the earth to stretch
open-handedly upward.

Attendants pushed it under the earth again but again it stretched
up toward the light. Finally the mother herself returned to the
grave and struck the arm with a rod, and the arm with its little
hand like a five-lobed leaf withdrew back into and under the wet
earth.

And yet we are not Afraid, some say trembling.
We merely imitate leaves of the Apple in wind
because we honor it as a mother, honor it as a child
should tremble before mother. We are not afraid
she said with a quaver in her voice,
pronouncing sad words to watch them float downward
from her mouth to the ground. Or was she blowing bubbles of
soap which caught the light (we say "caught the light")
which caught the light and tumbled through air to earth.

A thing to do with the mouth, profess:
there would be, will be again a season
when violets are dark, and darkly the hyacinths
bloom beneath some trailing vine. A girl will pick
me a crown of flower, flowers, and time will waste
us both and it will seem the world is home
again. Call it home.

Without being forgiven, released from the consequences of what we have done, our capacity to act would, as it were, be confined to one single deed from which we could never recover.

Hannah Arendt

"FOR THE RELATIONS OF WORDS ARE IN PAIRS FIRST"

For the relations of words are sometimes in oppositions.
For the relations of words are according to their distances from
the pair.

—Christopher Smart, fragment B, 4

Hear, and here is where it is spoken; some say
and sum up a kind of catalogue of self, a self
is a catalogue of lacks, some say as a catalogue of likes,
of nostalgias—
what was once and will not be won again

over the usual couplings in the night
against the light continue even this
                                        this night, tonight
these words are written; the rain
a spilling of kindness, a kind spell.

HEAR HERE

Any morning anyone—the sky and the sound
of birds, the air a river no bird can fly
through twice—an uneasy joke: the air's
a fluid like any lake or river's thrilled
hydraulics, streams and currents rising /
falling turbulent in the manner of, the mode
of mania … no; another try: the bird in the morning
like the boy striding like the sun the sense
of sun bestriding the eye the vision of the boy
who along the gray tiredness of road intently
walks watching the herons' murderous
intent wading along the stream which mirrors
the unintended path which the boy
follows that morning leaving (he
thinks) home as if the world waits. Invent.

An easy joke, but a tender thing he thinks
walking late that morning after waking from deeper
than usual dreams … deep in dream's welter a wealth
of peculiar banality … recalls the instant a worse
dream turned sexual inhabited still by
the weight of the normal … enormously waiting
versions of some self to inhibit that wetness.
Like a murmurous hall in which he is witness
of multitudes; murderous, fearful, and they
inhabit themselves their knowledge already now
whatever you, shameful, confess. Repress.

But what does it sound like, walking away?
A path metaphoric, a path of mind, a way
unintended, a glint in the ear of green heard
in the sound of the bird stalking fish sharp
of beak and tiny of eye, tiny black dot awake
in the face of the bird the white bird silent
in the morning at the edge of the water
which makes rippled noises which make in

contingent air a rippled path to the ear
of the walking boy afraid of his dreams
who thinks the world awaits awake as if
herds watch from the forest edge. Attend.

A HISTORY OF MORTALITY

The transition from childhood is death of the child
obsessed with butterflies with the moment
a worm becomes mind, Psyche,
brief a transition
a bird is also

and here is how disease is cured, was:
As for the living bird, he shall take it, and the cedar wood,
and the scarlet, and the hyssop, and shall dip them
and the living bird in the blood of the bird
that was killed over the running water;
And he shall sprinkle upon him
that is to be cleansed from the leprosy
seven times, and shall pronounce him clean,
and shall let the living bird loose into the open field.
Leviticus 14:6-7

What is a bird? A shiny animal
hard to the touch, but warm
and a potential pen to write with
like an angel, a little.

A bird is a kind of wish, but isn't
anyone's wish but her own, his,
but is still like a wish of a boy
who *would* move that way. Or a girl.

What a bird is is
like nothing but,
nothing. And there is no
other wish than flying—

the scandal of legs
to carry us, who have no feathers
and can only write wishes
like it or not.

The insects fly, many, some
and can be furry crawlers one day,
butterflies the next.

They know the code
but do not know they know

[a. L. *codex*, later spelling of *caudex* trunk
of a tree, wooden tablet, book, code of laws.]

And the light shineth in the darkness;
and the darkness comprehended it not

the word in Greek, comprehend, [katalaben],
second aorist tense, emphasis on punctilier action,
no regard for past, present, or future

What is a bird?

Between. (I know, knew,
a mathematics of "between,"
whose given terms were "point,"
"line," and "between"
then all derivatives therefrom …)

I am amazed
I said to no one in particular
the particles glinting as the sun
light picked out dust
in the air of the room
leaving the gloom of
corners alone
what I meant was
I am amazed how
human we are, we humans.

A maze quickly glinting in the light of sun
a trail through piled boxes books and papers
my fault, my glory,

I said "we humans" identifying
myself as one of those I spoke aloud as if
it mattered. The verb form of matter: "matter"—

we become identical through things,
we are identified, as things, and we are

how amazing
how we are mazes, boxes and particles
forming walls, arranging themselves
through light, chiaroscuro, the darkness dwelt.

Another time and the story would begin:
These things we leave behind he said
he left behind him things trailing
a trail breadcrumby of silver halides

(…the psychoanalyst's listening facilitates access
not so much to a latent meaning, but to a latent language…
                                        Before Words, A. DiBenedetto)

latent images, negatives, photo-
graphy, light writing…

(*For instance, Alice and Bob will interact in such a way that Alice is
able to "prove" her identity to Bob by convincing him that she knows a
secret without revealing anything about that secret.*
"Cryptographic Protocols, 5.3, Identification," *Codes*, R. A. Mollin)

the image waiting patient in the emulsion
was a crystal lattice of silver beautiful already
in the dark, potent, potential. Do the ill

still love us? the dying...?
They are too busy, distracted...actual, no
longer potential...but they are pictures
...can love continue in spite of sex,
in extremity, a code of flesh

We comfort our selves shamelessly
regard, regard, the birds leave
those feathers behind, a flurry of leaving,
flat miracles...not flat, curved
curiously aerodynamical.

THE CONSOLATIONS OF DEFEAT

The American searches
for an aesthetic all his own,
finally finds it—and all is Protestant after all,
denial and delirium
like shelter along the bus route,
the plastic hut where the poor
and huddled mass will wait, the bus
with its own name and number as if the path
were not a circle but eschatology

itself; not a circle
but you know what I mean:
if you fall asleep en route
you will still some time come back
to where you start. (see Eliot, his *Quartets*)

Might I quote myself? "a minor note, etymology—
Paranoia is *para* plus *nous*, mind…a parallel mind?
a second mind, being of two minds, being overly
mindful, minding manners: a matter of kind-

ness, and a manner of speaking."

"I have read—and I believe what I read—speakers
of Saherero have two front teeth removed
in order to pronounce properly (which they prefer
to chewing); here is aesthetic desire proved

to matter, a minding inviolate."

"In this preference for visual gaps over auditory—
indeed, even the tactile sense (is there a word
for the feel of food on the teeth? the story
of tearing with incisors is not so absurd)—

this preference

sacrifices for spoken soundings, abounding
dedication so deftly human, makes us cry
O for a life of sensation!" But sounding
The life of the mind-mangled implies

fear and a failing, all done—how often the dental
is the focus, the American's, the paranoid's last hope
or blame (a source of sound,
voices). Rhymes with mental.

You still will some time return to your start.
Where you were. This is so American, so much
like that wilderness we grew within,

as atonement. American atonement as aesthetic as,
as we dream of the jungles of Asia, dream of tigers
bright as childhoods, passing and repassing (we grew
within) on their daily rounds of jungle—we understand

the national need for a trail, a thread of bare
earth threading through. The smallest remnant.

NOTHING PRIOR TO ANYTHING

I had an idea—not an idea, less concept than notion (as in those objects around sewing, needles and thimbles) that a certain democracy of the interior is possible: human entrails indistinguishable were they offered to view, and elegant: glistening purples, greens, and reds—a complexity of reds must abound in there. Complicity of reds. I discovered the interior when my father took me to butcher our cow which had a name and history—she was my chore before school, her milking and feeding—but now was beyond freshening so was needed as meat. Men in aprons with knives in hand and each had dangling from his waist a sharpener which he would deftly catch and cross against his blade ritually swift and efficient. One placed the barrel of a small caliber rifle behind the horns of our cow and the muffled report was slight and the cow slumped briefly was hoisted rear feet first and began an arc suspended the most glamorous stage of which (evisceration) caused a great balloon of purplish gleaming to spill onto the clean floor to be quickly gathered by an aproned man. And there is mother of pearl, and the shine, the lustrous shine of lips, the edge where her warm mouth joins her lip, a boundary beckons and the gulf beyond: obscure interior. The allure of lipstick. The gleam of *cosmetic* akin to *cosmos*.

POOR IN WORLD

It is not enough not to be, it is the wish
to have never been that intrigues (confounds
erasure) and the quick equivalence (zero
as verb) or the wish it hadn't happened:

among the forms of suffering this takes
the cake: he said "Forget it" and I would
gladly, but how?

The attempt to forget activates
the dorsolateral prefrontal cortex while
the hippocampus goes dormant.
No guarantees—hard it is
and long the path to Lethe.

The past, since it does not exist, is
hard to erase. Tears and the gnashing
of teeth. You recall an ambition.

The ambition to have never been—o round
and round, ambient modes, the world rounds
a little sleep—lies and lies

strongest with the old and the very young.
Cover your tracks (path: Tao)

[1736 R. Brookes, translator, Du Halde's Gen. Hist. China III, 30
*Among the Sentences [of Lao Kiun] there is one that is often
repeated ...Tao, says he, or Reason, hath produced one, one
hath produced two, two have produced three, and three have
produced all things*] All is vanity, saith the Preacher

Ways to be done with and well out of:
the ambivalence of an early death,
or late agonies, declared interests,
declaimed selves, All that is not vanity

79

is erasure. Forget and forfeit/forgive.

Immer est es Welt Rilke wrote, and we can translate
as necessary, all that is is world. The world is, nothing
missing. Nothing past. But *und niemals Nirgends
ohne Nicht* he wrote, and never nowhere without
nothing—if only it didn't happen, or if only
anything could be forever healed.
I never spoke the language but read
Rilke as if someone's life could be saved.

SAD HOUSES

If some small mind among mountains asserts
a self (any self will do) and makes a home of height,
then it *says* a self out of hope and fair weather.

But weather is where we, in the end, live, and nothing
will do but to bend to it, and anyone's child is worth
dying for given circumstance, if you stand around long enough

you'll find some life to save, from drowning in something,
then if it is still day and the sharp angled peaks do not block
the sun the light will change, the trees will cast

shadows and point the way, a way, houseward, home.
I do live in this world's words, and those regrets did
follow me here, among mountains, the wildering

of place in the evening where nothing
substantial remains for long unbent.
Call it a kindness.

Delusions, hallucinations, agitation, blunted affect, social withdrawal,
apathy, anhedonia, poverty of thought, poverty of speech content;
affects the most fundamental human attributes including language,
perception and sense of self

Particle physics: the search for that which is only itself
and is not a randomness
not statistical terror.

For there is a dream from the adversary which is terror.
For the phenomenon of dreaming is not of one solution, but
many.

(Christopher Smart, Jubilate Agno (fragment B, 3)

Here is what I learned: a thing—a house, for instance—is
generated when matter (for instance, if you make a house,
timber, nails, sheetrock, tubes and tendrils of copper) is arranged
according to form (a plan, blueprinted architectural, for instance)
so when form dissolves matter might remain, but no house, no
place to return homeward. *An animal is generated when matter
(contributed by the mother) combines with form (contributed by the
father).* His theory, he wrote, and meant it, Aristotle. Not mine,
but meaning is meaning, take it, I said to myself.

*For the changeableness of changeable things is capable of all those forms
to which the changeable are changed. And what is this? Is it soul? Or
body? If it could be said: "Nothing: something that is and is not," that I
would say…"* here's a saint confessing, but does it help and who
wouldn't say it, that all is and is not?

The clouds were, and daffodils, and the work he did—
now no more.
His life, health and happiness. The weather, too, it is and isn't.

The known world's anguish increases, mentally creased and
spindled—how odd that *anguish* has nothing to do with
angle—to bend, as a fishhook … the words I mean.

*Forming connections with the cerebral cortex, white matter and
brainstem, the limbic system is involved in the control and expression
of mood and emotion, in the processing and storage of recent memory,
and in the control of appetite and emotional responses to food*

Well, and who doesn't love this summer weather?
But some do prefer the darker comforts
of hearth and the need for
and some prefer to walk
unswept autumnal
and some change their names
hoping to find one that fits
and a more savage substance
the body, fishlike, dangling
give it a name, a name

Bathed in tears the eye tries,
we have made the air dirty, and the water,
which is our house but we feel clean in our hearts
or no, we don't, we feel besieged and therefore
no longer look, "heart" being a metaphor in this case
for…we have forgotten. Necessity, perhaps.

No, "heart" has a long history of abuse. I mean the word,
but also the organ. Bathed in blood the organ beats
its low tune for a lifetime, then retires…we look there
or would look there, in there, except that the air
is dirty, and the water, and evening is far, and the morning,

even if in opposed directions, and as in swimming a river
the halfway point is where it does not matter what choice
we make, to return or to continue, is of heart, unhoused.

BIRDS FLY THROUGH US

Of any boy a story, of any girl, his kind, her kind,
his kindness gone and glory   all remains, all that
remains is a kind of glorious   grieving, a skill like any.

"If he had not had a house, where would he have raised his son,
and in what rafter would he have stuck the sacrificial knife?"
Kafka, "Abraham"

As boys they played, as girls   played again against
the will or wisdom of mothers,   others, there was a river
there where boys and girls   who play each the other

apart part   of growing up was pain and painful all
fathers say the sacrifice cry in the night the knife
cry I or Ai Ai   or some Greekish chorus cry

call of lament out of the night   the past of feeling feeding
for once and again against   aghast at what fathers do
must do to keep the kindly   household whole, budget

balanced, the orders.   Past what whimsy the past
too lived there no more   but he did, Abraham, obey
and lived after   so they say   with himself knowing

he would have cut   having loved god more than a son   how
fatherly is that   what boy as a boy I would play
and she would play and cry   and we had a house

and the river stayed where rivers should   and still
there was death and darkness to dream and a knife for guidance
good riddance a sharpness and a gleam like water

I see icy nights   ahead he said   he sadly
said to her in bed, in her bed
in bed a boy   and a girl and dread

Here is a story some Greek told: a father
had a dozen children each child had thirty
white sons and thirty black daughters
each died every day but became immortal

the word *fear* is related to *fare* and it fits.
To fare forth into the murderous day,
the far-bordered night. One of the ablaut forms
of the Aryan root "per," to go through
we go through days and nights, Time, timorous.

"There is an earthly house which sounds with a clear
note, a tone, and the house itself makes a music
but contains a silent guest and both
hurry onward, guest and house together—"
Flumen et Piscis, the twelfth riddle of Symphosius.

If we are afraid, his father said, of anything
we are afraid of everything, just not all the time.
Anything can be a weapon, any weapon can be
a poem: "when Cyrus invaded the Scythians
they sent him arrows, a frog, and a rat
Cyrus could read the message: unless
he could hide in a hole of the earth like a rat,
or in water like a frog, he would not escape
their arrows which would fall from air,
the sky no refuge, no border"

But the lovely fish, silent, who moves with
the water his house, which house is buried
in earth—not covered, but a long hole in which
frogs might live but are not silent—in which
rats might swim but are in but not of the house—
moves, is not afraid of water is of air, of arrows.

A writer named Wiser described the beheading,
of Landru the casual look the quick transfer
of a head severed dumped adeptly from
its basket into the casket to join rejoin
the body—the task of the headsman's

assistant, swift ritual after the blade's descent.
An interesting brief divorce, for moments,
measurable if few, head and body separate,
(the body rolled immediately off the machine
into the adjacent casket before the blade
ceased trembling) then introduced (the crime
of the one the innocence of the other) now
absolved, resolved. Remembered.

TENDRIL

et in Arcadia ego

Her House

I am the one satisfied with sadness,
summer on the river, her last house unlivable
(loved?) a wasp hive in the bird feeder a hive unhidden

a now-clouded plastic (to feed birds)
(a tube attached to the window) from
the kitchen a view of a lawn strewn
with calcium carbonate (not chalk,

limestone, cave stalactites, coral, or pearls) oyster shells
from her hen house, snakes in the nest box—

still this is landscape, still life: a torn scatter,
trees at the edge of woods seen from the road
a horizon broken … all is broken

yellow swirl in the green of rice are
the tops of crawfish traps in flooded fields
various shades of gray and blue varied angles

◆ ◆ ◆

of light—a textured wall a grain silo an evening

—a house to be broken a life too, soon

a second storey of a house complete, the first
story walls washed away all
tatters remain against posts and studs

(no, see—I saw this, the house standing
but the walls by the storm away   taken
a kind of neatness to it, unkindness)
the line of debris in the trees at twelve feet
the high the water at its highest a horizon
white trailers, hundreds ranks and rows among

a kind of wild hibiscus spider lilies
nests with herons   herons stand sentinel in nests

in trees along the road dense crowds of white and blue,

❖ ❖ ❖

                    (the former Louisiana heron
now tricolor) and cattle egrets

camellias, the smell
the barn house the pump house
water   rice   sugar cane
biplane flying, helicopter at rest
horses   sheep   goats
caterpillars crossing the roads

mirages and red wing blackbirds on the pavement
cormorants an alligator dead on the highway
Cameron, Calcasieu, Jefferson Davis, Vermillion
these the names of Parishes: Latin *parochia*, from Greek *para* +
oikia = "a temporary staying" (para, paradise, paranoid, etc.)

Indecent, the delicate exposure
of roots, pine and oak and other, torn great holes

❖ ❖ ❖

in the mud then dry white soil but now new rain
new larvae the mosquitoes drive us off the land
into her house where she has lived Faulknerian
thirty years in cool semidarkness
cannot speak nor swallow, tubed, ticking
clock-like forward into silence. She writes me notes.

Elegant analyses offered by wind thus
wilderness is one result, an end like an art form
the long walk homeward.

The wild deer-ness of the days and dense
city only distant, fair gossamer presence
our kind reward—the palpable
sensory, sensible night's eros.

Infant

Lacelike and loose, gossamer
goose summer, cobwebby, but wait for St. Martin's—November
eleventh and, if, fine weather—but snow to come, but not yet.
Not.
Of the past, the unspeakable haunting hinders
to hover this way above the page like pasturage is
to feel filled pleasantly unformed past or passion.
To speak is to wait for better weather,
to watch. Forget and fasten

to space opened there, thereby like small rain on the tender
herb she did alight and here or there
is nothing to be done a moment a

monument to, all monumental days accrue and nights,
consolations of offending vision ... she did not
stand near and seemed oblivious which was dear to him, his
sight, who watched for hope even of a tree cut down
that it will sprout again and that the tenderest branch will not
cease,

tender to only this moment, his century
not peaceful, his century a serious
deficiency, like memory as martyr—

❖ ❖ ❖

him—no, me—during his day. Mine. This
current lingering on a line, Child,
electric, instigation enters,
or not ... cows, for instance, walk
and eat simultaneous. Unhindered.
But do not speak.

What it means is, something
always hinders, someone, unless
a freeing like erasure lightens,
illumines, the path, the load.
To linger is to love. Live. Delay
departure till the cows
which cannot speak

come home. Clearly something
happened here. Cleverly. He had
"fair-feathered feet," not I. No eye
in that, there, to witness. Ill-formed
offspring of my feeble brain,
she said. Not me. Mine. This
speaking is all however,

From the Chapter "Jesus Speaks to Judas Privately"

There is this morning snow on the mountain visible
from where I, as a function of time and space—altitude
and season, and the biology of the eye—am. Morning
snow and the season beyond me an engaging agility
of mind, mine, and like privacy betrays itself.

"Step away from the others and I shall tell you the mysteries of
the kingdom"

"She was in the hospital for less than a month. During that time,
she remarked that she was the victim of an organization that was
placing photographic apparatuses into 'lightholes' in order to

obtain moving pictures of her. She said that things had not been
natural to her for most of her life, and she told a symbolic story
of two children who went into the woods and were varnished
by a witch so that they were like two dolls and couldn't move...
then she said it is not she who was varnished, but the rest of the
world, and that things did not look natural."
Admitted Oct 16, 1934, name withheld

but the staff called her Berenice, for obscure reasons,
and she was, in the fashion of the time, beautiful.
Anacreon says Eros is blond, and throws a purple ball
asking me to play... the rules will follow, first comes the game.

You would agree were you here with me, momentous
and monumental you. Companion, accommodative
or so I would wish you, wish you into existence.
Everyone says "you," writes "you." You do not.
Everyone is wrong much of the time, you say.

The mountain is not wrong. The mountain is distant.
The mountain is not a mind, the mountain is not
of mind, the mountain is my wish, is. I am.

"Step away from the others and I shall tell you the mysteries of
the kingdom"

You are still with me? Between you and me is a mile
or a wish. We always wished to be alone, we all.
A little of the snow sifts into the blue, the gray
blue air which makes the mountain transparent...
to appear and to parent, both now verbs,

but the mountain allows the light of sky to shine
through, a trick, the singular mountainous light
descends upon us liquidly until the day delights

alone. All one. The greatest betrayal happens
alone, always away from the others and when
the very light itself delights in it, it heals. Itself.

Delectable dialect. But my sins are small and
all I have is this mountain behind to betray,
so stay. You. Let us reason together.

Who isn't entertained by the sane, doesn't watch them out
walking in the cool of the evening, the sane, when they are
allowed by their keepers a little time to themselves, a little time
to think. These asylums are generally grand, well paved and
give onto views, as of ocean or mountain, horizons at any rate,
in all cases. Broken or smooth. The sane often amuse in spite of
themselves, without effort, seized by the moment. Amuses you?

Seizure, as in, to suffer one. Seize, to take
and eat, or use, at any rate, as one's own.
Livery of seizen, concept in law, an act
of delivery, livery. Asylum, a place where
you can't be seized, where the law will watch and wait.

When you were a child did you know some low thicket
where your mother could not see you
and you in shadow could watch at least
the feet of passersby, but to not be seen,
not be seen, there was no greater luxury,
to see and not be seen. Some would say.

"Step away from the others" he said and
we then walked a little together it was
pleasant since the season was transitional,
spring or fall, I cannot recall, and we spoke
of nothing that mattered, and the matter that
did, and some, I could tell, were watching as we walked,

and I liked that they might envy me (did you?)
since we were at a distance from them,
and we were close. Not you, but him.
Seized each by eros, his little games.
Or did you tell her, show her where?
I am counted among the sane, have a certificate, yet

this is what I feel: flesh, and a prickling along the arm
this which arm reach soon, would, toward
you, a frenzy might be but is not apparent,
and the organs such as heart and other, are
engorging. This is biology, health, and seasonal.
You are young. Never understand, stare at will.

I would write "sacred" for "scared" or sometimes
"scarred," and needed no analyst
since it was only an error. Eros.

In my reading, sitting under the magnolia
in late summer the gloss of shade occasional
parent passing beyond vision, I would marvel
at the notion that the king could not enter,
nor his men, the church to seize the rebel
knights, the heroes of my books.

"I had to recover the space
and give it symmetrical order.

I was walking." –Jean Daive, translated
by Julie Kalendek. I should know the French
and not rely on this carrying across, this.
But in that shadow, that shaped space
which is the wrongness of the best
translation, is asylum. The original
was wrong too. Eros. I was walking

no waking, and I saw her heard her
you, and I was taken by an insane wish
and counted it a betrayal of flesh to stay
alone but when I reached to *hold* and
caress you were the dream only,
varnishing, vanishing before reason.

Near Encounter

As the small rain upon the tender herb
she seemed to alight, and here is nothing
to be done about moments. All days
accrue and nights, conventions of
defensive visions—she did sit near
and seemed oblivious which was dear

to his sight, he who watched inspired
to hope even of a tree cut down
that it will sprout again, and that
the tender branch will not cease,
he thought, or would have peace

as he was his fathers's son, tender
and lovely only to his mother. His century
a serious deficiency, it is, his memory.

Tendril (A)

In the fall of that year I noticed a piece of a Roman wall now on
display in the museum. A relief panel in plaster. A bit of white
plaster had been molded in the form of a winged female figure
alighting on a tendril, set against the dyed blue wall while still
wet, the figure alighting between two deer. She, the winged one,
holds in her hand an offering to the deer she faces, a gesture
reminiscent of the angel by Klee who offers a little breakfast.

The wings are faintest curves, a series of streaks of plaster almost accidental. Love the accidental. The almost accidental. I could call those wings Aspects of Grace. They are not attached. They are suggestions.

Her curved body carved; to carve, a graph, engraved in plaster...

Seduction. I do not know if she is human, intended to depict the human form.

The Buddha and Heraclitus were contemporaries. The suggested curve between them in place and time. Only time.

I began making sketches of her, and her deer come to feed, in my notebook. I returned every day to make another awkward, personal version of a winged female figure alighting on a tendril. Some days I would get the line of the back, some days I would be able to imitate the wings. Never the entire figure.

As a boy I fell in love with a figure, a girl in a radio drama about a scientist who developed a microscope more powerful by a factor a thousands than any then known. In a drop of water through his lens he discovered a city in which lived a girl. As he watched the scientist fell in love then watched her writhe in agony and die as the drop evaporated. I had my own radio, my first transistor model. I listened to the story in the dark of my room.

An answer as an unfolding. To speak, for instance, to a figure with wings, and then to see the wings begin unfolding, as your answer. As in, "I love you" and she unfolds her wings to leave you.

Plicare. Replicate. Plait. Pleat.

I tried drawing her and am no artist. I filled a book, and then another.

Replicatory can mean, "of the nature of a reply."

I am no longer a child. Once we took our son to a little "nature museum" in Colorado. A tame deer followed us. We petted her, and were all of us humans shocked at how hard the hide was, how course the hair. Her little hooves were delicate, brutal.

Jean Cocteau adopted for his signature a five-pointed star, which he copied from the scar on Apollinaire's face. Cicatrix. Cocteau visited Apollinaire in the hospital—one of the Corporal Acts of mercy.

◆ ◆ ◆

algebraic curve: a curve expressed by an equation containing only algebraic functions, i.e. such as involve only addition, multiplication, involution, and their converses; of which kind are the various conic sections: opposed to *transcendental* (or *mechanical) curve,* one which can be expressed only by an equation involving higher functions, as the catenary, cycloid, etc. *curve of probability:* a transcendental curve representing the probabilities of recurrences of an event. *curve of pursuit:* the curve traced by a point moving with constant velocity, whose motion is directed at each instant towards another point which also moves with constant velocity (usually in a straight line). *curve of sines:* a curve in which the abscissa is proportional to some quantity and the ordinate to the sine of that quantity; so also *curve of cosines, tangents,* etc. See also ANACLASTIC, CATENARY, CAUSTIC, CUBIC, EXPONENTIAL, etc. etc.

Tender

like small rain on the tender
herb she did
alight and here or there
is nothing to be done a moment's
monument to, all monumental,
days accrue and nights,
consolations of offending vision … she did
stand near but unaware which
was dear to him, his sight, who watched
for hope even of a tree cut down   Job 14:7
that it will sprout again and that
the tenderest branch will not cease,

tender to only his mother, his century
not peaceful, his century a serious
deficiency, like memory.

Tendril (B)

I listened to the story in the dark in my room. I suppose I cried.
Children do.

"Replicate" can be pronounced several different ways—one of
these, as an adjective, can refer to an insect wing folded back on
itself. From the Latin plicare, to fold, also replicare, to unfold or
to reply. An answer as an unfolding. To speak, for instance, to a
figure with wings, and then to see the wings begin to unfold, as
your answer. As in, "I love you," and she unfolds her wings to
leave you.

I tried drawing her and am no artist. I filled a book, and then
another.

Replicatory can mean, "of the nature of a reply."

Never Odd Or Even

—a writing illustrated—

Never odd or even unusual—an ordinary
defect is adequate, is human:

lie down to start, or rather start to lie
and write it down. If you do get caught, just say
you're an art student making a film.

(428 reels of 16mm black and white composite   *Industry*
optical track (sound) motion picture film prints   *on Parade*
and one document box of episode descriptions.
americanhistory.si.edu/archives/d4507.htm)

A glister engineered, rows of glassware,
postwar excesses, a nation gleams
emergent into the light, the light of its own
consumption…and boys before the TV
watch, waiting to emerge.
Butterfly from chrysalis, enrobéd.

Gen 39:12 And she caught him by his garment, saying,
Lie with me: and he left his garment in her hand,
and fled, and got him out.

The little god eros
gathers himself his qualities and offers a site—

who could resist this kind of pastoral
a clean well-lighted field for anyone

from the little gods there is a world
take pictures and liberties
pose yourself your friends

So, you know, here is a direction: once
Copernicus said you are not the center
he meant the planet itself (and yet
here is a cosmic system of which
we are the center: the entire
observable universe—if we speculate
beyond our vision we lose our place)

and then Darwin said, You are not
the apex of your kind, when by kind he meant
all life, at least, all visible life; you are not
an end, and then came Freud
who said, you are not in control,
you may not even be you, whoever
you are you cannot know except
you are not of your own life Author...

the mitochondria within, that's me,
too, and like a bigger god who has lost
control I only look, imagine looking,
and hope. Health. Viral vision.
If every cell in my body is also me
then all death is suicide... natural causes.

Nothing is numberless. All
is accounted for, every sex
is accurate. Now and again. Again

for instance any maker, for instance
the brick maker "a man entirely capable
of living a pointless existence"
(Monarch Notes to *Heart of Darkness)*
Poet, Greek for Maker, bricks, too. A word a mirror
of every other—this is the only rule.

Which mirror matters? Lighting is life.
A reasonable facsimile. "What is the difference"
the crude man asked "between the erotic
and the pornographic?" I do recall.

Bricks without straw was another question

but who can walk past a mirror without
a peek, a sly sideways cast of the eye
as if this time to surprise, in error…

silvering it is called but the metal
is mercury, or was once. The manufacture
of mirrors was darkly
held, a secret. Making mirrors
engaged the best minds, the darkest,
glittered against, no *with* the waywardness
of flesh, filled the hours the darkening
and forewarning hours

there is a reason to calculate,
the rock against the glass shatterable
consider the concave with its arrowed engagement
of light focused and the boys of the neighborhood
looking into homemade cosmologies,
homemade pasts, members of the club.
Astronomy too is making

a series of further "humiliations"
analysis situs;

the world's first photograph:
pewter plate treated with bitumen of Judea
then washed with oil of lavender and white petroleum, in
Ste-Lou-de-Varonnes, by Joseph Nicéphose Niépce, 1826,
then lost for a hundred twenty six years…

"in the name of your Lord who creates humankind
from a blood clot…he
who taught by the pen—taught humankind
what they did not know"
is the translation I read, from Qur'an—God
is the common name for everything…the

ordinal number, unimaginable, the arrogance
of enumeration, The Numberless infects
the night (thighs glisten, angles of incidence
equal angles of reflection) stars

Barbara DeGenevieve wrote: *If you have a "Night Vision"*
setting on your camera, you won't need lights.
The effect is eerie but very beautiful.

How to make your own
erotic movie. Dot com. Never odd
or even strange, just true is the trick. To life.

For your class project. It works.

Tendril

It can happen that a man will wander every day
to the same place in a museum and look
for no reason he can say at the same small
image a few minutes at a time it makes
this day a day of some moment
he regards his day his momentary delay

he is not a monk he might have been
were he less tender toward himself, stranger.

❖ ❖ ❖

Vulning is a word. The flag
of Louisiana includes a pelican vulning, feeding
her young her blood her self-inflicted wound;
self-infliction is a tendering of
the self: maternity allows it, the breast.
The pelican is no mammal but feeds anyway
her young from her breast, at least in Louisiana
on the flag a blue field tendered

tendere, L stretch.

tener, L delicate

❖ ❖ ❖

There is an order of nuns known as
Sisters of the Holy Face. St. Cajetans
only recently a Saint, was Blesséd (Gaetan Catanoso).

❖ ❖ ❖

tension, tender, tendril, attend:

(if you come at night, like a broken king   (T.S. Eliot))

catenary, "famous curves index," Jasper Johns'
chain . . . a shape is firm in the mind, a curve
which can be described by a formula . . .
you can look it up, the shape a chain takes attached
on two ends, free in the middle. Gravity
has its hand in, a manner of speaking.

❖ ❖ ❖

my melisma . . . Felix Mendelssohn letter 1831
melos, song / melody
neuma, pneuma, a musical sound in tenth century, and the
breath of god

(for spirits when they please
can either sex assume, or both; so soft
& uncompounded is their essence pure   (Milton))

❖ ❖ ❖

the beds I sleep in, all narrow
slender as necessity; dream

gowns with straps like strings breakable
flesh embedded
the fabric film and depth of light on the pillow case
the lids of whose eyes transparent;

I have never seen the work of Chris Parsons, known as
"lawn artist" who works in dew with brooms sweeping
patterns visible for minutes until the light which makes
visible makes invisible the dew which while refracting
photons succumbs into vapor.

The dew is vulnerable, the boy sleeping the girl sleeping are
vulnerable, to wound and be wounded, wound
in sleep which has elements, requirements and rewards.
"To sleep together" as tender anxiety,

as consciousness (the French for "conscience")
reaches tentative into the dark, dark tendril
of self twines and the other who shares, say,
a pillow will not yet speak of dreaming
too easy and tender to mention.

Hard to the Touch

What is a bird? A shiny animal
hard to the touch
a potential pen to write with
like an angel, a little, and lives by
a lake a lake a blueness
lake and wind the wind the
blueness of wind glasslikelake
glass birds on the blue
a kind of wish but isn't
anyone's but her own
but is still a wish of a boy
who *would* move that way.
He said in love with Piper

who has never spoken to him
but blows glass like wind
across the lake no
the boy blows glass Piper
turns the tube control
in her voice says Blow
says Softer says Stop.

What a bird is is
like nothing but,
nothing. Softer
as glass warmed
to a toffee slow swirl
invisible made to obey.
And there is no other wish than
the scandal of legs
to carry us who have
no feathers and can
only write glasslike.

The insects fly, many,
and can crawl one day,
be butterfly the next.
They know the code,
but do not know they know
[codex, later spelling of caudex
trunk of a tree, wooden
tablet, book, code of laws.]

I am amazed I said to no one
in particular the particles
glinted as the sun
light picked out dust
of the air of the room
leaving the gloom of
corners what I meant was
I am amazed how
human we are, we humans.
A maze quickly glinted in
the light of sun a trail through piled

boxes books and papers
my fault, my glory; glass
birds shatter. What is a bird
of glass? Only if it can fly.

❖ ❖ ❖

A Standard Clarified Nomenclature of Disease, (N.Y.:
Commonwealth Fund, 1933): sZ, Simple, hebephrenic, catatonic,
paranoid; involutional melancholia;

(Varnish, ORIGIN Middle English : from Old French *vernis*, from
medieval Latin *veronix* "fragrant resin, sandarac" or medieval
Greek *berenikē*, probably from *Berenice*, a town in Cyrenaica):

1929: Diagnosed sZ, 1950: Developed memory deficits 1967:
Markedly impaired memory, but no delusions

…my predicament was that of a committed illusionist in an
environment that was officially dedicated to the eradication of
illusion   Hollis Frampton, photographer

Káthodos, or, Original Sin

Descent of the soul, the fall; the fear of fallenness

Of the Past, the Unspeakable

A kind of haunting hinders him—
no, me—during his day. Mine. This
current lingering on the line, Child,
electric, instigation enters,
or not...cows, for instance, walk
and eat simultaneous. Unhindered.
But do not speak.

What it means is, something
always hinders, someone, unless
a freeing like erasure lightens,
illumines, the path, the load.
To linger is to love. Live. Delay
departure till the cows
which cannot speak

come home. Clearly something
happened here. Cleverly. He had
"fair-feathered feet," not I. No eye
in that, there, to witness. Ill-formed
offspring of my feeble brain,
she said. Not me. Mine. This
speaking is all...

however, to hover this way above
the page like pasturage is
to feel filled pleasantly
unformed past or passion. To speak
is to wait for better weather,
to watch. Forget and fasten
to space opened there, thereby.

Repose

The tractrix is the evolute of the catenary,
these names of curves being what we love...
geometry becomes us, our essential sadness

such as *asymptote*—aligning
the unbearable vision with bearable
desire, a kindness of geometry.

"Catenary" was invented in the Age of Reason,
the word and the concept, but not the shape. Or yes,
a shape can be invented. From Latin *catena "chain"*

the name *tractrix* was coined ("Coin" from the Latin
cuneus, wedge, then cornerstone, (not to mention the vulgarism)
then die (as in, device for stamping a coin))(the path

of a word trailing along a horizontal history) by Huygens,
who also invented the clock. Imagine a boy pulling
a stone on a string, the string a little longer

than the distance from the boy's hand
to the sidewalk. The stone bounces a bit
on the concrete, makes a satisfying clatter,

background noise to the boy's thinking,
if thinking is the word—something more like
reflecting, from the Latin, "to bend."

His mind was bending, as if to the magnetic field
of earth, the very earth. The mind a magnet.
Any boy or girl would bend. That clock had a pendulum,

a weight on a string, like a stone to touch to try
to touch the earth the desire of each for each,
stone to earth. A distinction allows *sensuous*

to be about touch, as in the stone at rest
a sensuousness of stone, grave, of earth;
allows *sensual* to be of sex ... *sensuous*

invented by Milton (1641), an attempt
to avoid the sexual overtones of *sensual*.
Somewhere must be other forms of desire,

other shapes than sexual. Pointless, maybe,
the distinction. In "Figure Drawing for All"
Andrew Loomis described (in words) before drawing

the reclining female nude, how the parts
of a body which can move will assume prettier poses
than in their upright modes. Shapes assemble into

larger shapes, lines linger into lyric. Pendular
parts draw the weak mind of the boy in the night
who has no other object to align, who leans

over the borrowed book in moonlight.
I used to live in a body. I now am that body,
not inhabitant. An intricate intrigue ... imagine a people

wander the hillsides at whim, urge flocks
to wander with them, follow seasonal
impulses. The people are the landscape, as are

animals and plants and air and sidewalks.
The study of the tractrix started with a problem
posed to Leibniz: *What is the path of an object dragged*

along a horizontal plane by a string of constant length
when the end of the string not joined to the object moves
along a straight line in the plane?   —*Famous Curves Index*

Some sources for the language of this book:

The Origin of Consciousness in the Breakdown of the Bicameral Mind, Julian Jaynes. Houghton Mifflin, 1972, 1990.

The Oxford English Dictionary. i.e.: House "...Goth. *–hus* (known only in *gudhûs, temple,* the usual word being *razn*). The ulterior etymology is uncertain: it has been with some probability referred to the verbal root *hud-, hûd-* of *hydan to hide.*

Collected Poems of Sir Thomas Wyatt, (Harvard University Press, 1950).

Memoirs of a Proof Theorist: Gödel And Other Logicians, Mariko Yasugi and Nicholas Passell, a translation of *Gödel,* written in Japanese by Gaisi Takeuti.

"The golden verses of Pythagoras. Translated from the Greek, by N. Rowe, Esq; With A poem on the late glorious successes, &c. and an Ode for the New-Year, MDCCXVI. By the same hand."

1,2,3...Infinity, George Gamow. Viking Press, 1947.

The Duino Elegies, R. M. Rilke, various translations into English.

If Not, Winter : Fragments of Sappho, translated by Anne Carson. Random House, 2003.

The Self-Dismembered Man: Selected Later Poems of Guillaume Apollinaire, translated by Donald Revell. Wesleyan, 2005.

Hysteria, Christopher Bollas. Routledge, 2000.

Nehemiah 2:7: Moreover I said to the king, If it please the king, let letters be given me to the governors beyond the River, that they may let me pass.

Thinking in Pictures: and Other Reports from My Life in Autism, Temple Grandin. Vintage Books, 1996.

Diane Arbus: a biography, Patricia Bosworth. Norton, 1995.

The Human Condition, Hannah Arendt. University of Chicago Press, 1958.

Ovid III: Metamorphoses. Loeb Classical Library, Harvard University Press, 1977.

Before Words: Psychoanalytic Listening to the Unsaid through the Medium of Art, Antonio Di Benedetto. Free Association Books, 2005.

Codes: The Guide to Secrecy from Ancient to Modern Times, Richard A. Mollin. Chapman & Hall/CRC, 2005.

The Poetical Works of Christopher Smart, edited by Karina Williamson. Clarendon Press, Oxford University Press, 1980-1996.

Lectures of R. L. Moore on Point-Set Topology, University of Texas, Summer 1961.

"Birds Fly through Us: Arches," Ronald Gonzalez. Welded steel, glass, wire, slag, metal filings, rust, bird nests. 2000, Laumeier Sculpture Park, St. Louis.

Disappearances, William Wiser. Carol and Graf, 1992.

Ordinary Choices: Individuals, Incommensurability, and Democracy, Robert Urquhart. Routledge, 2005.

The Natural History of Mania, Depression, and Schizophrenia, George Winokur, Ming T. Tsuang. American Psychiatric Press, 1996.

http://www.history.mcs.st-andrews.ac.uk/curves/curves.html

http://www.tertullian.org/rpearse/manuscripts/gospel_of_judas

http://www.nationalgeographic.com/lostgospel/_pdf

Coherence in Psychotic Discourse, Branca Telles Ribeiro. Oxford University Press, 1994.

To Will H. Low, Robert Louis Stevenson.

Some of these poems have been previously published:

"Six Scandals," "Last Days of Gödel" in *French Connections* (ed. Galineau and Bedell)

"Eclogue" in *The Laurel Review*

"Social Conscience: Well Meant" as a broadside by *Empyrean Press* (Sharon DeGraw)

"Pharmaceutical Sanctity" in the journal *26*

"Yeats Was Asked to Write a Poem about the War" in *Tin House*

"Animal Intelligence" in *Matter*

"Resemblance," "Gregg Shorthand Dictionary" in *Coppernickel*

"Tea Party" in *Public Space*

"Sympathies," "For the Relation of Words are in Pairs," in *Bayou*

"Nothing Prior to Anything," "Hear Here," and "Poor in World," in *Tarpaulin Sky*

"Performing Art," "From the Chapter 'Jesus Speaks to Judas Privately,'" in *Thuggery & Grace*

"Birds Fly through Us" "Repose" in *Zingmagazine Chat*

Bin Ramke has written eight
previous poetry collections.
He holds the Phipps Chair in
English at the University of
Denver, and he also teaches on
occasion at the School of the Art
Institute of Chicago. In 1978, he
was awarded the Yale Younger
Poets Award. He grew up in
east Texas and south Louisiana.
He has been a teacher for more
than thirty years.

THE OTHER

OTHER BOOKS BY ROBERT DANA

POETRY

The Morning of the Red Admirals   *2004*
Summer   *2000*
Hello, Stranger   *1996*
Yes, Everything   *1994*
What I Think I Know: New & Selected Poems   *1991*
Starting Out for the Difficult World   *1987*
In a Fugitive Season   *1980*
The Power of the Visible   *1971*
Some Versions of Silence   *1967*

PROSE

A Community of Writers: Paul Engle
& the Iowa Writers' Workshop   *1999*

Against the Grain: Interviews with Maverick
American Publishers   *1986*

LIMITED EDITIONS

Hard Candy   *2008 (chapbook)*
Wildebeest   *1993 (pamphlet)*
Blood Harvest   *1986*
What the Stones Know   *1982*
In a Fugitive Season   *1979*
Journeys from the Skin   *1966 (pamphlet)*
The Dark Flags of Waking   *1964*
My Glass Brother and Other Poems   *1957 (pamphlet)*

THE OTHER

ROBERT DANA

ANHINGA PRESS
TALLAHASSEE, FLORIDA 2008

Cover art: *The Mask,* by David Alfaro Siqueiros
© 2008 Artists Rights Society (ARS), New York / SOMAAP, Mexico City

Author photograph: Peg Dana
Cover design, book design, and production: C. L. Knight
Type Styles: titles set in Lithos Pro; text set in Adobe Caslon Pro

Library of Congress Cataloging-in-Publication Data
The Other by Robert Dana – First Edition
ISBN – 978-1-934695-07-4 (paper)
ISBN – 978-1-934695-08-1 (cloth)
Library of Congress Cataloging Card Number – 2008931768

This publication is sponsored in part by a grant
from the Florida Department of State,
Division of Cultural Affairs, and the Florida Arts Council.

Anhinga Press Inc. is a nonprofit corporation dedicated wholly to the pub-
lication and appreciation of fine poetry and other literary genres.

For personal orders, catalogs
and information write to:
Anhinga Press
P.O. Box 10595
Tallahassee, Florida 32302
Web site: www.anhinga.org
E-mail: info@anhinga.org

Published in the United States
by Anhinga Press
Tallahassee, Florida
First Edition, 2008

For my beloved, indomitable Peg,
one more time

ACKNOWLEDGMENTS

Abalone Moon Journal (webzine): "And Everything Will Slowly, Slowly Happen"

Another Chicago Magazine: "Everything in Its Own Green Time" and "October Glory or Duster's Song"

The Chattahoochee Review: "Passages" and "Solving for X"

The Georgia Review: "Looking for Shark's Teeth" and "After the Storm"

The Hampden-Sydney Review: "Going Back" and "Taking Down the Christmas Lights"

The Iowa Review: "Alive," "O, The River is Deep and the Water is Wide," and "Elegy for a Hometown"

New Letters: "Except"

The North American Review: "Still Life with Dust & Deep Summer Shadows"

Pif (webzine): "Mending Art" and "What It Was Like Before Dark"

The Prairie Schooner: "Here Come the Roses" and "Ora Pro Nobis"

Runes: "Notes on What's Drifted Away"

The Tampa Review: "A Flashguide to Florida Shorebirds," "The Other," "Thorns," and "Whelk & Line"

Weber Studies: "Beach Attitudes," "Morning, Taos" and "The Other Side of the River"

TABLE OF CONTENTS

Great nature has another thing to do
To you and me. ...
— Theodore Roethke, "The Waking"

MORNING, TAOS

The desert pigeons dance on the grass,
And in the time it takes one cloud to pass,
Beneath the dry, immaculate blue,
Nothing thinks of me or you.

1. THE OTHER

THE OTHER

The myriad green leaves
spackled with blue
as if the sky were laid on
rather than back behind,
and the whole illusion,
by a simple lift
of the pillowed head,
moves up and down
through the slatted blind
as if seen through
a shuttered lens.

And waking this way,
one sees how easily
the skin of the real
is slipped, peeled
into abstract beauty
or a terrible unfamiliarity,
that makes the hair
bristle on the neck
and the heart skip fast.

The morning radio's
bombers, murderers,
drunk behind the wheel,
on prayer or sacred
hashish, or brute vision,
and bent on blood
and terror, seem not
to see how wide
this world is for error,

or this Other
disdaining all we are,
glorious or embittered.

ALIVE

A taxi full of blood.
        Wallpaper of amputations and bandaged children.

*

War, assassination, mass murder, and murder are the bread
        of our days.

Who will not speak of it?
        Who will not?

*

May they never know sleep.

May they spend their old age weeping and weeping and weeping.

May they hear the rhyme rats hear before they die.

*

Sweetness of oncoming spring curdles.

*

We waken each day
        drugged to dullness by repeated acts of savagery.

Imping mortality.

*

O walk me again, Friend,
          under the red and gold of Woolworth's Five and Ten.
Past the Tangee.

                    The moon and stars of Evening in Paris.

Bottles of Carter's ink
                    — Sunset Red, Sea Green, Midnight Blue.

And boxes of deckle edged writing papers.

                    Embossed envelopes lined in gold a boy might envy.

                              *

Lead doughboys and ceremonial hussars.

                              *

The counter girl who asks, smiling, "May I help you?"

                    And she could, but neither of you is certain how.

                              *

Soft silence of summer afternoons.

                              Cloud-throated.

Every sense alive.

And the voice in your ear saying,

"Never tell anyone your secret name."

EXCEPT

The river in full flood,

            flashing and roiling and muddy.

              And it's only late February.

How many tons of silt moving?

         How much nitrogen every toxic mile?

*

In town, where the water whirls swift under the bridges,

      a hawk hangs in the high air.

              Blunt broadwing.

*

And in the woods behind our house,

        the sharp-shinned posted high in a bare oak.

*

      Gardens truckling under the ruck and rot of winter.

*

All of us waiting.

        Except the river.

EVERYTHING IN ITS OWN GREEN TIME

North of nowhere,

And the long cold spring is finally ending.
        Spiked with purple iris.

                    Great clouds lofting and sailing.

*

No wrens bubble and sing from the roof of their old house
                                this year.

But behind the near cherry,
        in a mulberry
                storm-twisted and gangly and barely leafed out,

        a pair of jays,
                sharp-faced, feathered rips of the sky's blue,

feed and warm their babies.

*

This morning,
        a week before Memorial Day,

I've already pruned the blown lilac blossoms,
                    the lavender and the white,

while back in my little New England town, in a later spring,
                    their scent blows

sweet and heavy among the flagged graves.

Old veterans, what's past is past.
                                    The Old Glory.

                    *

I weed and mulch the iris,
        and rake the dirt in the lettuce garden with my hands.

I sprinkle the fine seed in short shallow rows, and cover it,
                                            and water it in.

Black-Seeded Simpson for Pop,
                my funny, potbellied, machinist foster father,
                                        long dead now.

And Mesclun for myself, lost in the future.

                        Was it parsley for remembrance?

                    *

At the end,
        I think I'll know how it goes.

                    *

I'll bind up the wounds of my poems
            and hum them to healing
                        under cool white sheets.

A glass of clear water beside each bed.

I'll switch off the lights,
(Good night! Good night!)

the book breathing shut behind me.

*

And hard starlight will flood the room.

WHAT IT WAS LIKE BEFORE DARK

Rain-light and rain.
                       Late afternoon.

       And just beyond my kitchen window,
                    two young deer the color of fallen leaves

pass slowly through the green and yellow paisleyed air.

     Big ears flicking. Pausing. Turning to look at one another.

They've come to graze
           my neighbor's last frost-sweetened windfalls.

Golden Delicious.
                  Dozens a-bubble in the clipped grass.

I grow older as I watch them.
                      Count the apples.

AND THE REST WILL SLOWLY, SLOWLY HAPPEN

Jumbotron vistas.

A hullabaloo of clouds.
Long brushy strokes of grey over peach and gold.

*

Looking up, you know it.

You don't drill through *this* mountain.
And this sky doesn't end with the heavens.

*

Reading others,
here in the dry and perfect air,

I hear the old, tired, elegant cadences; the familiar, sad narratives.

Still others, their voices miked and shrill,
straining farther and farther out
for what's closer and closer home.

There's another music in this buried light.
Feral. Free ranging.

Hush.

*

A young, yellow-legged hawk,
slender, unperturbed, perches on our fencepost a few feet away

before gliding out,
                low, over the rabbit-brush.

                              *

Early evening, our neighbor skunks,
                          wagging their ostrich-plume tails,
            forage dropped wild apples in the yard,

and prove not everything here is turquoise, beige, or rock red.

                              *

"… the vast marvel is to be alive," D. H. Lawrence said,
                      who lived up mountain an age ago.

"Start with the sun," he said,
                "and the rest will slowly, slowly happen."

                              *

                Soul-ju-ju in the ground.
                                    Evening lightning.

Tape-delayed thunder.
                      Little drum-dance of rain.

AFTER THE STORM

Snow sealing off the high passes and the wind howling.
Snow plastering pine, fir, and spruce.

                              Capping the river rocks.
Stubborn boulders scattered in the icy, black flow —
                    anchored by their own hard gravity.

                    *

This morning the valley's grey and white.

          I'm reading Libbrecht's *Field Guide to Snowflakes*.

Studying the beauty of ice.

Mastering its terms: bullet, needle, capped column, rime, star —
          and the importance of dust
                              in turning water to crystal.

               Outside, the banshee of driven snow wail past —
                              wraiths tall and twisted.

                    *

None of this will help you
                    posthole your way out of a frozen wilderness
                              of deep snow —
Long's Peak west,
               the Mummies to the north, curtained —

All landmarks,

little codes and semaphores of animals and birds blotted out.

It won't even help you shovel your walk.

       I think of summer in the Never Summer Range.

            *

Never mind that
       when I'm here alone,
           silence is the language I speak most often.
I have its grammar down by heart.

       It glides easily on its own melting.

            *

Now, another day.

The morning fire in the grate flaps its tongues,

                          gossiping,
    and the wind palavers in a loose window sash.

And miles away the high white peaks fume and gleam in the sun.

TAKING DOWN THE CHRISTMAS LIGHTS

Our neighborhood's gone dark again,
all its Christmas lights down now.
We unclipped from our eaves two
weeks ago in the unseasonable, late,
December warm, thirty yards
of blue icicles, accordioning them
into fist-sized bundles, securing them
with green plastic ties, the kind
meant for staking up garden
plants in summer, then packing them
neatly in a box marked *Outside.*
Our P-E-A-C-E sign with its mad
racing combinations and slow fade-
out-fade-in hangs blankly green
once again for another whole year
with the tools in the garage: crowbar,
loppers and pruners, step ladder.

And tonight, the season at last grown
wintry, knuckles cracking with cold,
my wife coils up snaking extension
cords and dismantles our white,
skeletal, antlered reindeer, Horatio
— he of the moving head — last
and best of show, folding him down
and packing his separate parts
into his proper carton for storage
in the basement, along with boxes
of bulbs, strings of lights, tree
ornaments, some with family histories.
And the two small, robin-sized,

feathered birds, one red, one white,
that top our tree as shining spikes
and stars and archangels do others' —
the one descending, the other rising.

2. BEACH ATTITUDES

WHELK & LINE

Inside the whelk shell chapel,
in the whirl and shatter of colored glass,
                              sailboats heel on blue waters and red,

      under off-center angular bursts of the sun,

fired by the actual sun of ten a.m. more fiery and fiercer still.

            Twist.   Furl.   Spiral.

                              *

                              Outside again,

                  lowly librarian of leaves,

      I watch them release, soundlessly,
            from the high-storied trees.

Watch them drift down softly,
                              brown and dry,

onto the grass, into the parking lot, into the street, into winter.

                              *

                  Mysteries of sleep and fever.

                              *

Wherever you are,
                  line is the way the wind blows.

A FLASHGUIDE TO FLORIDA SHOREBIRDS

Morning.
    Old pungencies of wrack & weed.
Gulf waters flat.
      Grey green.

Dolphin cruise the shoreline in the rain.

The beach,
      empty but for one old man
& the crowding, indifferent seabirds feeding
  at his feet —

willets, sanderlings, gulls,
        a cripple-footed turnstone.

Overhead,
   cousin to the pterodactyl,
        eons removed,
   eleganced now & easy,

a pelican slips
    across the long currents of the wind.

       *

By afternoon,
    the sun lavishes itself again
on Toy Town
on The World Capital of Ticky-Tacky.

At the club,
        horseshoes sail and ring,
                  ring and clank
and ring again.

"Oh, perfect!"
        a woman's voice shouts from the turquoise pool
beneath the tall & glistening schefflera,

speaking, almost surely
            (instinct without history)
    of nothing.

Or of the past,
        which always is.

PASSAGES

Mr. Cormorant walks the morning beach —
       a long-billed cap,
          a muscle shirt,
             and a bad hip —

his right hand closed on a silver jingle.

*

A flock of little seabirds rises at his approach
    and flees
         out over the shimmering water,

            dropping toward it like black shot —

at the last minute lifting
         and turning,
       then returning in a dash and tumble —

white confetti flashing down the shore.

*

Whispers of passages. Debarkations.

*

The Compass and The Rose.
Boatyard shambles of rumpled metal and bent pipe.

*

The yellow sailboat —
                    Unlucky Lady or *Moonshadow* —
                              driven ashore in a gale here two weeks ago.

Aground now in four feet of water.
            Bottom ripped out.
Stripped of gear by her skipper and left.

Rock steady,
            she moves not at all in the heavy chop,
her mast and stay still tall and straight.

The one true cross.

                              *

This sea 'samite sheeted and processioned' —
                    Oh yes, Hart, you had that right.

And hurricaned.

                              *

Honey light.
            Late late afternoon.
                              A long ribbon of fragrance.

A bald man among the strollers.
                    Surfer shorts business blue.
                              Cigar Cuban.

Redolences of Papa and Gregorio.
Of Fidel and Raul and Che high in the Sierra Maestre.

Of fingers gifted to wrap the bright leaf.

*

Sharp, sad airs on a gringo guitar.

*

Star-scratch and black velvet.

Wash and flapdoodle of shallows.

And the spirit,
    megametamorphic,
        hies itself home.

LOOKING FOR SHARKS' TEETH

Back home,
>> ninety-degree heat.
>>>> The sun punishing the roses.

The blooms of Honey Sweet blowtorched and blown.
>> Cherry Parfait melted,
>>>> like a bride's hankie gone limp in the rain.

*

Here, the marvel of waking.

Pour and tor of moonlight on the sea.

>> It comes over me sometimes,
>>>> like a love of shadows.

*

Or body surfing in my aging wreck of bones,

>> wave-battered, and drifted standing
>>>> in the riptide,

heavy boots of water dragging at my legs.

*

The sun has no ethic; the sea, no morality.

What did you expect?

A lecture on the politics of pleasure?

A love letter written on air?

                              *

Better to look for fossilized sharks' teeth in the runback of low tide.

Glossy black points in the argument.

                                        Or many-colored sea glass
along the tide line,
            misted by a hundred thousand tumbles.

                              *

            Yards away,
a five-year-old blonde stick of a boy shouts insults at the waves,
        slapping at them,
                    holding out his arms,

            the water barely past his knees.

                              *

Our day is what it is
                    under the clouds, the streaming kites.

Among the red-yellow-green-and-blue-striped umbrellas.
Amid the busy little encampments of beach chairs.

Sweet. Lucky.

BEACH ATTITUDES

Blessed is the beach, survivor of tides.

And blessed the litter of crown conchs and pen shells, the dead
blue crab in all its electric raiment.

Blessed the nunneries of skimmers,
scuttering and rising, wheeling and falling and settling, ruffling
their red and black-and-white habits.

And blessed be the pacemakers and the peacemakers,

the slow striders, the arthritic joggers, scarred and bent under
their histories, for they're here at last by the sunlit sea.

Blessed Peoria and Manhattan, Ottawa and Green Bay, Pittsburgh.
Dresden.

And blessed their children.

And blessed the lovers for they shall have one perfect day.

Blessed be the dolphin out beyond the furthest buoy,
slaughtering the bright leapers,
for they shall have full bellies.

Blessed, too, the cormorant and the osprey and the pelican
for they are the cherubim and seraphim and archangel.

And blessed be the gull, open throated, screeching, scolding
me to my face,

for he shall have his own place returned to him.
And the glossy lip of the long wave shall have the last kiss.

3. LOSSES

ORA PRO NOBIS

Morning.
                A sunless, grey December day.

Dark confetti of starlings fluttering onto the power lines
                                along Interstate 380.

              A black paragraph,

                          broken,

unreadable.

*

My sister, the nun, is dead.

We're on our way to the airport to fly to Boston to bury her.

My thoughts walk in old shoes.

*

My sister, The Great Complainer,
                  vexed her whole long life
                      by the imperfections of the world.

Our imperfections.
                Yours and mine.

Once in love with a red-haired boy, she married God instead,
whose candle never flickers.

*

Perhaps that's what her saints and martyrs were.

Our great complainers.

Glorious scolds.

Stinging us to madness until we stoned them to death

or burnt them at the stake

or drove them railing into the desert.

*

Plain in her open casket.

Not serene.

Tidy. No martyr, she.

"She isn't there," my eldest daughter said.

Like the husk of the locust after the locust has gone.

We've all seen them.

Accidentally.

Clinging to the bark of a tree.

Perfect, thumb-sized sarcophagi,

translucent and empty.

The grinding, loud song gone

that fired so many shimmering summer afternoons.

Or like this vacant wren's nest,

blown from our cedars by yesterday's bitter wind.

Less than a handful.
                          A weave of little grasses,
trailing some child's lost, iridescent, party streamer.

                              *

It's 3 a.m.

        I take my consolations where I can.

        In the winter dark,
                      in the steady breathing of my sleeping wife.

        In the humming of my cat, Mr. Tunes —
                        small, solitary, grey singer,
              blessing the water in his bowl.

QUERY

For RM

My cat ate a wren this morning, one of a pair.
He seemed just to take it from the air.
Now her mate is cleaning out their nest,
From some sense that starting over's best,
Or from grief, or rage.
                              Is he bitter,
There among her fine, disordered litter?
I hear a puzzled query in his song,
About where she's gone, and for how long.

THORNS

A week into spring,
        already this morning I've shed blood in the dirt,

        blood on the young leaves of the roses.

                Living Easy's canes thick as your little finger

and studded round down their entire length
                        with Jesus-sized thorns, hooked and cruel,

                bring it to the fingertips.

                                *

Where no man's word is good,
        the air yellows and thickens,
        the seasons accelerate, swing, jar,
                                temperatures rise.

The line chokes with paper forms, petty signatures.

Our rich talk leaks away into micro-babble.

                                *

Old Adversary. Boa constrictor.

Never the viper or the adder,
                        a flick of the merciful poison.

        No.

Slow lurker in the weeds.

Old suffocater.

Hug it to death. Squeeze all freshness from it.

Godsend to those for whom all sentences diagram.
And mother to the box,
                            the safe, the tried and true, the old ways.

The mighty and the high.

*

                        All that righteousness
gone out the chapel door in a little box of dust.

*

Requiescat, old girl.
                        Twenty-three skidoo.

*

Now the deck's glassy with long-awaited rain.

The downpour thrums,
                        fades,
                            drums down again, the spring leaves

doing their green trick in the cold.

A wet robin seeks the deck rail,

                       shakes his coat dry like a dog,

                             and is gone.

             *

Underwaterlight now.
Murmur of thunder.

                  I try to name what we need.

             *

Blessed are those the rain falls on.

THE OTHER SIDE OF THE RIVER

So I'm half-Irish, half-Italian.
                              A Gemini.

          Two operas. One for each head.

                    The first, dark and sad.

                                        The other, a bluster of light.
                         Spectacles.
          Not stories.

                                        *

Nature passing through us all. Wind through a screen door.

                                        *

The other side of the river,
                    my old friend,
                              wicked competitor,

mind that moved words as surely as a surgeon his knife,

          sinks daily deeper into dementia.

                                        *

This afternoon, rereading his poems,
                    I see how nothing blatant troubles them —

          no mother-murderers of their children,

no stink of sweat,
no mill hands swilling down shooters at the end of the day,

no dead mule in the cane rows.

*

Money, that subtext of palm trees and dust.
Most distant of stars at the moon's eclipse.

*

Still —
troubles enough to order a life.

A world unsatisfactory.

Made beautiful, occasionally,
by a blues tune, the memory of a girl's white breast,

wild asterisks of sunlight on the water.

An aunt, an uncle, an old house on a dirt road.

*

And now, he's going down hard.
And slow.

*

May 21st.

A chilly, grey morning.

Cottonwood seed sailing down like snow,
whitening the lawn, gathering into little drifts along the drive.

Then the 8 o'clock tumble up the sidewalk —
of first grade boys barely as big as their book bags,
past our maple, past the lilacs,
loud for their bus.

Is there, among them, a Spinoza? Mickey Mantle?

*

Catkins.
Pollen, dried to yellow mud
and crusted at the edges of deck planks and patio tables.

No answer
from the high wind wild in the oaks, hickories, cherries.

No answer from the large, black eyes
of the barred owls down the creek.

Cold night filling up the ravine.

INTIMATIONS OF AUTUMN

In memoriam: Donald Justice, 1925-2004

The weather have overcasted.
        And the sun have borne off some with some clouds.

            And them peach colored trumpets,
them daylilies is blaring out some ragged jazz,
        just low enough for bees and such.

                            *

And yesterday beside your casket,

                                graveside
where I honored you with your own words,

I dressed in Fifties academic livery
                        — the seersucker jacket,
            light blue button-down Oxford-cloth shirt,
                            a tie.

            But with a difference.

The tie was Henri's.

            Not the lovely lavender Countess Mara he bought
                        in a haberdashery on Rodeo Drive,
the last time I saw him alive —
                the one he bought to impress his psychiatrist,
                a woman he'd fallen in love with.

            (Oh, mellifluous Henri! Easy for heartbreak.)

No, not that one,
>   but a cheaper silk rep (7.50 the tag still says),

>   black,
>   slashed by gold and dark red stripes.

I chose tan slacks slightly frayed at the hems of each leg
and socks worn thin at the heels.

In memory of our modest beginnings.

A time when mothers darned and mended.

>   *

In our America,
>   immigrant girls still grow taller and more beautiful
than their lost parents could ever have imagined.

>   *

Dear friend,
>   while you were dying,
>   I walked an empty morning beach in North Carolina.

Across the Intercoastal Waterway,

>   I could hear the WHOMP WHOMP of rockets
slamming into their targets at LeJeune,
>   the pop of chopper blades.

Back at the rented house,

the resident barn swallows sliced the air
                    above the sea oats and shrinking dunes,
            the hot macadam of the drive,

skidding,

        flittering,

                    coasting up gusts.

Perfect and oblivious in their sheerness.

                    *

I see

        the sea I have loved is too large.

            My smaller spirit cannot fill it.

                    *

            I make this wish for myself and for you:

A high sky.

            An intenser, deeper blue.

SOLVING FOR X

       Wild October wind, and Indian summer flaming out
leaf by whirling leaf,
           flake by tiny flake
                      in winks of early snow.

                    *

And up the road, in a small Iowa town,
               my ex-wife's dying ounce by ounce,

      wasting away with cancer
in the same red house we lived in thirty-five years ago.

                    *

What did she truly love, I wonder now.
                    Her demons?

    I'd bite my tongue through before I'd say so.

    But the shadow of the brother who dazzled her father's eyes,
and died his freshman year in college,
       leaving behind an endless season of grief —

a gloaming like the granite light of this autumn day — ?

                    Who knows?

                    *

Why can't I now recall
                a single, special, joyous hour,
one not framed and frozen in Kodak black and white?

In twenty years, there must have been some.

        The births of our children.
                                Her grittiness in Mexico
(Muy differente Americana! they said)

                when we bucked our gringo landlord and moved
lock, stock, and suitcase out of his elegant house,

lime tree in the courtyard,
                scorpions under the Spanish tiles —

        into Carmencita's parents' dirt floored hospitality.

Then all of us to the house off The Alley of the Fireworks Makers.

                                *

Later, the angers and disappointments,
                                betrayals, blame, recriminations.

        The world heaving and cracking.

                                *

The silence between us has lasted more than thirty years.

Too late now to have that civil conversation
                         about all the things that really matter.

Cheated soul,
          you've other more serious work to do.

                    *

Did we, like so many others, mistake the destination for the journey?

                    *

My own bitterness dissolved long since,
                         like a snowflake in the rain,
I wish you peace.

          Peace.

O, THE RIVER IS DEEP AND THE WATER IS WIDE

I'm sitting at the Rose Garden Café in my front yard,

my half-blind, ailing, small grey cat
   snoozing on the flagstone path beside the flowers.

*

This morning,
     mid-September,
          autumn's come early,
clad in naked air.
       An edge of winter to the light.

The iron smell of snow in it,

          although the sky's cloudless,
and the trees still green with the leaves of late summer.

*

I might be in the mountains of Thrace,
         or that little town in Corfu,
   Pelikas,

sipping gritty black coffee in the stony square,

   the sunlight sweet with the scent of cold pressed olives.

The whisper on the lips of it.

*

Perhaps if I walk far enough now,

                    listen hard enough,

I'll hear it again,

           put it in my pocket and carry it home.

         *

O, the river is deep

          and the water is wide.

OCTOBER GLORY OR DUSTER'S SONG

Back home,
        our October Glory maple turns,
                    day by day,
     from within,
          glowing,
until the whole fire-balloon of it bursts into flame,

      the embers of its burning leaves,
         ticking down, one by one,

        onto the still green grass.

               *

Here,
      the mountains, snowy and cloud-flagged,
        astonish us.

The wind crashing down narrow canyons,
      chewing dust and foot-trails,
         buffeting windows and doors,
     the chimney damper clanking all night long.

               *

I put my faith in strong coffee, good bourbon,
               and the next two minutes.

               *

Left to myself a few days, I live cheap.

I hike,
read my eyes dry, watercolor badly,
        and try to teach myself to pray as my old cat does.

At first light,
                an aria of hums and rumbles.

Later, a song to food and fresh water.

                A little vesper hymn, perhaps,

as the valley slowly fills with darkness.

MISS FUTZY ONE LAST TIME

"You must stop your sobbing and weeping,"
      she says in her ruined meow,
      "And make yourself stone.
Dig in deep and hard with all your ten nails,
and make your nine pounds count for fifty,
and when the drugs take you down at last,
      show your little teeth."

4. GOING BACK

GOING BACK

Will it be like home or one foot in the grave,
when I return to my little New England town?
I live now between the mountain and the wave.

What will I lose? What will I save?
A boyhood autumn, red-gold slanting down?
Will it feel like home or one foot in the grave?

Admit it. You've sometimes been a slave
to memory. The girl, the dance, the gown.
We live between the mountain and the wave.

Let Rip Van Winkle once more dream and rave
in his old horse-trough by the library, his frown
hawking apples and one foot in the grave.

Mac, Ju-jic, Honey, Ruth and Dave
are gone now, into the sear and tumble-down.
We live between the mountain and the wave.

The mill run's coppery. Wild waters don't behave.
A fly drifts, dazzling brook trout and brown.
Does it seem like home or one foot in the grave?
I live between the mountain and the wave.

NOTES ON WHAT'S DRIFTED AWAY

September, 1949.

        GI college boys.

                (Government Issue, that is.)

      Still wearing the white t-shirts, crew-cuts,

              chinos we'd mustered out in.

Luckies tucked tight in the rolled up sleeve

      in a style James Dean would make famous years later

              in *Rebel Without a Cause.*

           *

Already rebels, we'd had the cause.

           *

     Stardust and *Autumn Leaves.*

                Velvet Fog.

Sartre. Camus.

        Fuck your beanies, buddy.

           *

Now,

      existential carpenters on the roof, clawing and hammering.

Casals sawing away in stereo

        at Bach's Cello Suite No. 2 in D minor.

Me, thinking in no particular key whatever
                    of Tom Dunn's Crit class.

                              *

Signs.
        Symbols.
                    Semiotics. Old magic in new bottles.
        Or vice versa.

                              *

McManus, sarcastic and fastidious. Argumentative, ever.
                                   Van Laningham,
        blonde, ruddy-cheeked,
                    local boy from the right side of town.

And Jonesy — Robert Usher — black, from Corinth, Mississippi,
                    the most talented writer of us all,

who sentenced his stories to years of hard labor
                    in Henry James's old clothes.

        And me, thinking in no particular key whatever.

                              *

The mind in the act of creating the landscape out the window.

                              *

Pert bird.
Proud sparrow.
Commoner.

*

Young men, met only for a moment
        and its momentary purposes.

  Magicked away in one intense breath into their lives.

Hey-ba-ba-a-rebop.

    Then, silence.

*

  A whole half-century gone in an eyeblink.

MENDING ART

A long fall.

Our winged whimsy, Art,
        sailing above the kitchen soffit atop his little figured house,

a lopsided star above leaping orange fish and green waves in front,
        a sea scallop in a heart out back —

penates of culinary skills and poetry —
                                went crashing yesterday,

                nudged by a shadow.

                        *

All those divine powers gone smash in an instant.

        One black clodhopper,
his star wand and the raised arm that blessed all below with light,

his round head with its hair shocked outright,
                                his whole riven body,
        rivering across the floor.

                        *

        It's a frail music knits the world together.

A little god made of sticks and paint. Ruddy cheeked and cheerful.

Sailing up

on awning-striped wings.

All,
       deceptions of distance,
              distortions of perspective.

Holding his small head in my hands now,
          I see his eyes are wide, his cheeks pallid,

    the perfectly round mouth shaping a single frozen note —
Oh! — of — is it fear or surprise — ?

O O O O!

*

    Rainy, grey, and cold.
          September.

      A week's gone by, and this morning it's still evening.

The god's head and star-wand still drift the kitchen counter.

His torso, one splintered leg, and his raised arm
    lay morgued in a cardboard box on a worktable in the garage
         waiting for the miracle of reassembly.

So far all glues have failed.

    I think this god is made of alder wood.

Or apple or elm.

A grain that doesn't bond.

*

Shadow sits in the window now.

A flute warbles on the stereo from some far symphonic arbor.

I study the sodden trees, silvered leaves.

And I think about kindling a fire in the fireplace
                                    to drive the chill off,

to sweeten this empty neighborhood with smoke.

HERE COME THE ROSES

Here I am again
on my knees in the dirt.
Talking to the flowers.
Talking to the weeds.
Sweat pouring down my face like tears.

There are worse ways to go.

*

94   96   99

Day after day for months. And no rain.

Ten drops early this morning.
Next to nothing.

The trees drop their leaves like yellow coins.

In the countryside the crops are burning.

*

But here come the roses,
blooming by the bushelful

despite the heat that pinwheels their petals back
and clips short their days.

*

Pink Portrait and Country Dancer and Spring Morning,

Cherry Parfait, all lipstick and cream.
                              Oklahoma shedding red velvet.

Neon orange Voodoo atop its long rip of thorns.

                              Fourth of July's ruffled cockades.
         White Medallion.

Lighting up this neighborhood of sizzled lawns and wilting bushes.

                              *

This is what the bulldozed and burned groves of trees say.

The paved-over farms.

The poisoned air and water talking.

                              *

Our story's broken.

All I can do is piece it together.

                              *

I write it out. I erase it. I write it again.

Coralville, Iowa. Mid-morning. A long summer of drought. 2005.

The birds have stopped flying.

STILL LIFE WITH DUST & DEEP SUMMER SHADOWS

1. *CARP & DRAGON: DIRGE WITH SMALL BELLS*

Little Emperor,
                    my cat.
          I will not mourn you here in Beijing,
far from home.

          I will not add my tears
to the green waters of No Name Lake,

          flashing,
                              now here, now there,
its thousand silver scales
                              in the morning sun.

2. *RED DUST*

Our sweet houseguests gone now,

          the stillness you left behind blooms enormously,

a cosmos, or caul I'm the only human inhabitant of,
                              a blown -chute collapsing,

                    *

We buried you a week ago,

in that corner of the garden where you leaned like a railbird
                              through long summer days —

clocking ground squirrel and wren,
                                scholar of daylily and hosta.

A lion's eyes,
                yellow and clear.

                             *

Your final months, diabetic and blind,

        your once sumptuous grey coat gone ruddy
                                and silver and thin —
    little soldier of rags and patches —

        the words I spoke in another language in another country
meant nothing to you.

Your needs were water, food, sleep,
                                the touch of hands.

                             *

Some mornings on point,
                    one tufted, bleeding foot lifted,

the hunter you always were,
                    but hearing only the sound of gloved applause
your sparrows made
                    flushed from bushes —

your head still tracked them true,
                          as if you'd God's own ears.

           *

                      I stand here without you now
on the cracked drive of this house of deep summer shadows,

as I often shall until, as the old ones say,
                          kingdom come.

           *

And far, far to the west this morning,
      the red dust of China falls on snow in the high Sierras.

ELEGY FOR A HOMETOWN

           I'm done now with the dark houses of the East.
My hometown.

        The book is closing on my generation.

        *

Skinner satin mills
long gone to producing brass & machine gun clips
                & milk bottle caps
        are now themselves long gone.

And the orchard of 10,000 apple trees
           that fed our insatiable boyish hungers —
    a wilderness of stumps and weeds.

        *

Even the river's changed course,
        leaving Walpole's cove bleached & dry, where, in winter,
local farmers sawed thick blocks of ice,

      skidding them up a frozen ramp to waiting wagons,

horses named Belle & Sophie stamping & steaming & shaking
           their harnesses until they rang.

        *

My Polack neighbor's dairy farm's now a golf course,
        tees & greens & easy fairways.

We once killed black snakes there through the long summers
                & forking up corners,
saved the sweet-smelling, windrowed hay from oncoming rain,

    chaff stinging our sweat drenched bodies like shirts of nettle.

*

So what's to say when a whole chunk of your life
                      comes up missing?
You say to yourself, "Well, there it is."
              Or. "Well, there it was. Wasn't it?"

*

God's his own voyeur.

*

After more than half a century,
      I walk the town with the only man who knows my name.

*

Soon, I'll bury my own shadow & slip away like sunlight.

*

Simplicity's what I'm best at.

*

In the end,
a small box of a house by the sea.

       No electricity.
               No running water. Dirt floored.

Prayer,
      wind & slapdash from the whereafter.

NOTES

WHELK & LINE
The whelk shell chapel is on the campus of Randolph-Macon Woman's College, Lynchburg, Virginia.

PASSAGES
Hart Crane, American poet. Died 1933.

INTIMATIONS OF AUTUMN
Henri Coulette, American poet. Died 1988.

MISS FUTZY ONE LAST TIME
Miss Futzy, our green-eyed, "clouds on milk" cat, star of my post 9/11 poem, "This Time" published in my previous book, *The Morning of the Red Admirals.*

ABOUT THE COVER
Many thanks to Donna Sellen of Atlanta for the gift of the limited edition lithograph "The Mask," by David Alfaro Siqueiros.

ABOUT THE AUTHOR

Robert Dana was born in Boston in 1929. After serving in the South Pacific at the end of World War II, he moved to Iowa where he attended Drake University and The University of Iowa Writers' Workshop.

His poetry has won several awards including two National Endowment for the Arts Fellowships and The Delmore Schwartz Memorial Award from New York University. Retired from teaching after forty years as Poet-in-Residence at Cornell College, he has also served as Distinguished Visiting Writer at Stockholm University and at several American colleges and universities. In September 2004, he was named Poet Laureate for the State of Iowa.

His earlier books include *What I Think I Know: New and Selected Poems; Yes, Everything; Hello, Stranger; Summer;* and *The Morning of the Red Admirals.*